eco **books**

eco books

Inventive Projects
from the Recycling Bin

Terry Taylor

LARK BOOKS

A Division of Sterling Publishing Co., Inc.
New York / London

Editor:
Amanda Carestio

Assistant Editor:
Beth Sweet

Technical Editor:
Annie Cicale

Art Director:
Stacey Budge-Kamison

Design:
828 Design

Illustrators:
**Annie Cicale and
Orrin Lundgren**

Photographer:
Stewart O'Shields

Cover Designer:
John Barnett

Library of Congress Cataloging-in-Publication Data

Taylor, Terry, 1952-
 Eco books : inventive projects from the recycling bin / Terry Taylor. --
1st ed.
     p. cm.
  Includes bibliographical references and index.
  ISBN 978-1-60059-394-9 (alk. paper)
  1. Bookbinding. 2. Books--Format. 3. Handicraft. 4. Recycling (Waste, etc.) I. Title.
  Z271.T39 2009
  686.3--dc22
                                        2009003823

10 9 8 7 6 5 4 3 2 1

First Edition

Published by Lark Books, A Division of
Sterling Publishing Co., Inc.
387 Park Avenue South, New York, NY 10016

Distributed in Canada by Sterling Publishing,
c/o Canadian Manda Group, 165 Dufferin Street
Toronto, Ontario, Canada M6K 3H6

Distributed in the United Kingdom by GMC Distribution Services,
Castle Place, 166 High Street, Lewes, East Sussex, England BN7 1XU

Distributed in Australia by Capricorn Link (Australia) Pty Ltd.,
P.O. Box 704, Windsor, NSW 2756 Australia

If you have questions or comments about this book, please contact:
Lark Books
67 Broadway
Asheville, NC 28801
828-253-0467

Manufactured in China

ISBN 13: 978-1-60059-394-9

For information about custom editions, special sales, premium and corporate purchases, please contact
Sterling Special Sales Department at 800-805-5489 or specialsales@sterlingpub.com.

 This book was printed on recycled paper with agri-based inks.

contents

700 pounds of paper?

Are you surprised to learn that the average person consumes approximately that much paper a year? I was. But then, I thought about all the paper products I use in the kitchen and the bath, from the office to the mailbox: magazines, tea boxes, wrapping papers, and last night's take out. It's even more astounding to consider that of those 700 pounds, approximately 40 percent typically winds up in landfills instead of being recycled and reused. If you're mathematically challenged, that's 420 pounds of paper each of us needs to recycle in some fashion. That, dear reader, is a heck of a lot of paper.

I confess: I've always hoarded interesting bits of paper for future projects, and I have the boxes to prove it. Lately, I've been enchanted with a particular brand of tea with artful designs unexpectedly printed on the interior of the box. I find myself picking up oddly shaped, discarded boxes on the curb just in case I might have some use for them! You understand those impulses, don't you? And recently I've been avidly examining my recycling bin with more open eyes, as well as being more mindful of what I throw into my trash bag.

Please, don't feel guilty about adding to your average allotment of paper consumption by buying this book. Why? First, you're intrigued with paper and making books or you wouldn't have this book in your hands. Inside you'll find an array of ideas and inspiration for creating books using recycled materials—from paper to wood, fabric, metal, and more. And second, this book isn't printed like most new books: it's printed on post-consumer-recycled paper using agri-based inks.

The 40 books on the pages that follow are made using both familiar and not-quite-so-familiar book structures such as the folded Fold-a-Book (page 46) or the Branching Book (page 80), based on a palm-leaf prayer book. The simple pamphlet stitch is used to assemble pages in many of the books, as is the beautiful and flexible Coptic stitch. Throughout this book (and at www.larkbooks.com/crafts), you'll be amazed at the resourceful and creative choices the artists have made. From used printing plates to discarded dental floss containers, egg cartons to cassette tapes—anything that is tossed away can be imaginatively recycled into a book or a container to ship a book in.

In addition to great projects, you'll encounter all kinds of real-world information throughout the book. Read about Taller Leñateros (page 42), a workshop in Mexico that transforms what others throw away into beautiful paper and books. On page 78, you'll meet Jim Croft who takes green to new levels with his hand-powered self-sufficiency in food, fuel, and bookmaking. Learn about the inspiring possibilities creative reuse centers are providing to artists and crafts people around the country on page 23.

In our excitement at putting this book together, we accepted too many projects to fit into a mere 144 pages. For instance, I was inspired to make a book using materials a friend uses to draw and paint on: carefully washed, dried, and neatly refolded coffee filters. What's the perfect match for coffee filter pages? Well, burlap coffee sacks, of course, which I cadged from the local coffee roaster next to the bakery where I get my morning cinnamon bun. We're offering the directions for my book at *www.larkbooks.com/crafts*.

So go sort more carefully through your recycling bins (and your neighbors'), get your materials together, and make yourself some Eco Books.

basic tool kit

Most of these common tools are probably already in your household or crafting stash. They're basic and versatile tools that you'll need for making almost any kind of book. If you don't want to buy the tools you're missing, in many cases you can make do with something else.

Bone folders are one of the most essential and versatile bookmaking tools. They come in a variety of lengths and thicknesses and are made from actual bone or synthetic materials like plastic; some have a special coating so they don't leave shiny places on the paper. The pointed end can lightly score paper for neat creases while the dull-edged flat blade is useful for sharpening folds. In a pinch, you can use a table knife or similar instrument to help you make sharp, crisp folds.

Awls are primarily used to punch holes in page signatures and have a thin, tapered metal shaft with a wooden or plastic handle. If you don't have an awl, try a large upholstery needle, a sharp nail, or an old-fashioned ice pick.

Waxed linen thread is used for stitching books together. It is coated with wax, has a slight gloss, and cuts easily without shredding at the tips. It comes in a variety of colors and plies (2-, 3-, 4-, 7-, and 12-ply) and can be split if necessary. You can also use unwaxed linen thread, upholsterers' thread, buttonhole thread, or carpet thread, and wax them yourself or use them as they are—just make sure the thread you use doesn't stretch. Thread, twine, or yarn from other projects can be reused, too, but make sure it's strong enough, especially if your books will be used frequently (such as journals).

Large-eye needles are useful when you're stitching with waxed linen thread. If you have already pierced all the necessary holes in the page signatures *and* the cover, blunt tapestry needles work great. If your materials aren't pierced, upholstery needles are what you'll need. Be aware, however, that large needles leave large holes. Smaller needles make more delicate holes but can also break easily. Try multiple sizes until you find the right combination for your needs.

Craft and utility knives aren't interchangeable—and you should have both. A craft knife has a fixed blade and looks like a scalpel; it's good for cutting lightweight materials. A utility knife (a.k.a. box cutter) has a retractable blade and is best for cutting heavier materials like thick cardboard and leather. Make sure you have lots of extra blades on hand and replace them often as you cut, especially when working with heavier materials.

Rulers with a metal edge are very useful, especially the ones with both metric and English measurements. They're handy for scoring a long straight line or tearing pages cleanly against the edge. Cork-backed metal rulers won't slip and slide as you work.

Scissors of all sizes are always in demand. Make sure to sharpen them occasionally; nothing is worse than trying to cut with dull scissors.

Last year's phone book doesn't have to go in the recycling bin. Save and use it in a variety of ways. Open up the pages and use it as a punching cradle when piercing holes in page signatures, or tear out pages to protect a surface when you're brushing with glue.

Pencils are indispensible for marking. Nothing marks better than good old #2's, but everyone has a personal favorite. You'll need a good sharpener, too.

Polyvinyl acetate (PVA) glue is old-fashioned, clear-drying white glue. It does not emit harmful fumes, dries quickly, and cleans up easily with warm, soapy water. This glue remains flexible and doesn't become brittle after it's dry, which makes it ideal for bookmaking.

Small brushes are useful for spreading glue. Round-tipped glue brushes are great, but the inexpensive flat brushes made from synthetic fibers that are found at hardware or paint stores work well too. Rinse them after each use so you don't find a dried-up, un-useable brush when you need one.

Binder clips can be used to temporarily clip together a stack of papers, such as page folios. You'll find them in an office supply store (or perhaps you can liberate a couple from your office).

Self-healing cutting mats are optional, but they're nice to protect your dining room table when you're cutting with a craft knife. Alternatively, you can cut on old magazines or a phone book to protect your work surface.

A corner rounder is a type of paper punch that rounds off square page corners. An optional tool, heavy duty rounders can be a bit expensive, but there are cheaper handheld ones available as well. Corner rounders can be found in office or art supply stores.

Half-a-Dozen Book

Designer: Erin Zamrzla

Foam packaging takes hundreds of years to break down in a landfill, but this project offers an eco-friendly and artful way to reuse egg cartons.

Creating the Cover

1 If you are using a foam egg carton, wash it carefully with warm, soapy water and let it dry.

2 Use a sharp utility knife to carefully trim the top from the bottom half of the carton. Also, trim the tab flaps from the bottom half. Save the extra pieces for use later.

3 For a dozen-size carton, cut the bottom portion of the carton in half, creating two equal parts.

4 Trim any protruding parts so that when the cartons are facing down, they lie flat against the table.

5 Turn one carton face up so that it is in a landscape position. Decide which edge—left or right—will be best to bind to the pages (spine) and which will be best to glue a closure tab to. Once you decide, turn the carton so that the spine edge is to the left.

TIP: Every carton is different. Foam is extremely fragile to work with, so use the strongest side to bind the pages. Paper is stronger and more flexible to work with, so you have more options with a paper carton.

Making the Text Block

6 Use the scrap paper to create a template for your pages. Because every carton is different, you must create a custom template to work with your cover. Fold an $8\frac{1}{2}$ x 11-inch (21.6 x 27.9 cm) page in half. Lay the folded edge on top of the cover, placing the folded edge along the spine. Trim the template so it will fit within the edges of the cover, about $\frac{1}{4}$ inch (6 mm) less than the length and width of the cover. Your template will probably be around $3\frac{3}{4}$ x $5\frac{1}{2}$ inches (9.5 x 14 cm).

7 Carefully cut open the brown paper grocery bags and lay them flat.

8 Unfold the template. Cut the brown bags into pages the size of the opened template. Keep in mind the grain of the paper. You will need to make 36 pages.

9 Fold each page in half, smoothing each fold with the bone folder.

10 Nest together three folded pages to make 12 signatures.

Finished dimensions
6 x 4 inches (15.2 x 10.2 cm)

Materials
Cardboard or foam egg carton, either one dozen-size carton or two half-dozen-size cartons

Piece of $8\frac{1}{2}$ x 11-inch (21.6 x 27.9 cm) scrap paper

4 brown grocery bags

8 matching $\frac{1}{8}$-inch (3 mm) round eyelets

Cardstock (if using a foam egg carton)

100 inches (254 cm) or more of 4-ply waxed linen thread

Scraps of chipboard or cardboard

Tools
Basic Tool Kit (page 8)

$\frac{1}{8}$-inch (3 mm) hole punch

$\frac{1}{8}$-inch (3 mm) eyelet setter

Small piece of wood

Tapestry needle(s)

Sandpaper (if using a foam egg carton)

Stitch
Multi-needle Coptic stitch (page 134)

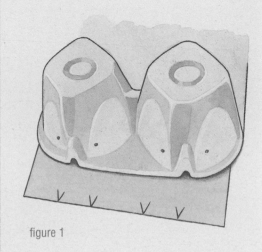

figure 1

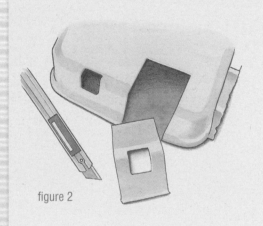

figure 2

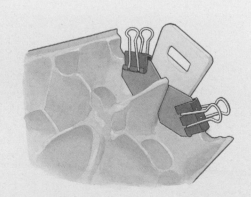

figure 3

11 Refold your template and place it back on top of the cover. Use a pencil to draw round corners on the template that match the curves of the cover.

12 Use either a corner rounder or scissors to round the corners of your template along the marking. Using the template as a guide, round the corners of the signatures.

13 Place the template back on the cover. Determine where to punch holes—a sturdy spot, if possible—in both the cover and the template. Mark four holes in the cover and four holes along the folded edge of the template (figure 1). Use the same steps to mark holes on the other cover.

14 Use the hole punch to punch holes in both covers at each mark.

15 Set an eyelet into each hole, making sure that they face out. Place a small piece of wood behind the eyelets while you set them. For foam egg cartons, you must take an extra step to reinforce the hole before setting the eyelets. Cut 16 circles from the cardstock, each about ¼ inch (6 mm) in diameter. Punch a hole in the center of each reinforcement piece. When setting the eyelets, place a reinforcement piece on either side of the carton to strengthen it.

16 To punch holes in your pages, open up the template and fold it so that the marks are inside the fold. Place the template in the center of one signature. Working on a cutting mat, use the awl to punch straight down through the signature at the four marks on the template. Be sure to punch directly through the fold. Repeat until all the signatures are punched.

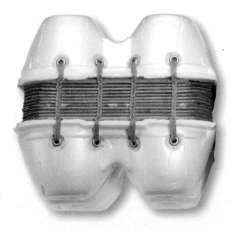

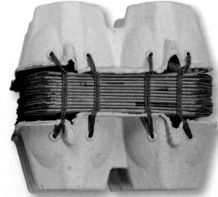

Assembling the Book

17 Bind the book using the multi-needle Coptic stitch.

18 When attaching the covers, tie a knot where the cover connects to the pages for extra reinforcement. This should alleviate some of the tension from the thread pulling on the cover.

19 Once the book is bound, add a tab to the edge of the cover to hold it closed. Begin by closing the book and measuring the distance between the top and bottom covers (the text block thickness).

20 Use the utility knife to trim the leftover pieces from step two into a tab and hook closure (figure 2). The pieces will need to overlap the same distance as the measurement from the previous step.

21 Attach the tab and hook closure one piece at a time. Apply glue to the edge and set the piece in place. Press firmly on the glued area for a minute or two, or until the glue is set. For paper cartons, allow the glue to dry completely, about an hour or two. Once dry, you may adjust the closure piece as necessary.

For foam cartons, you must first use sandpaper to gently roughen the surface area that will be glued, both on the tab and hook pieces as well as on the book cover. The glue will not hold if the surfaces are too smooth. Cut small scraps of chipboard or cardboard to place on both sides of the tab and hook closure pieces. Sandwich these pieces around the glued area and clip them together (figure 3). Allow the closure to dry for several hours before removing the clips and chipboard pieces. Once dry, be careful with the closure piece, as the foam may crack if it's bent.

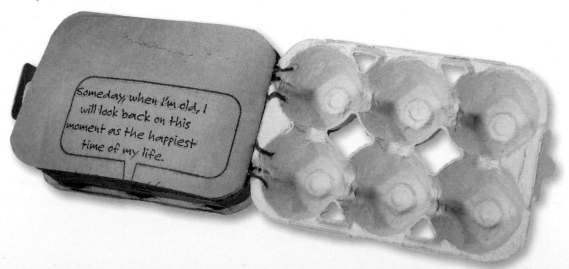

Someday, when I'm old, I will look back on this moment as the happiest time of my life.

Manila Folder Album

Designer: Geraldine Pomeroy

Stitched together with traditional Japanese stab binding, discarded office file folders get an upgrade to keeper of treasured family photos.

Making the Text Block

1 Cut off the lip of the manila folders, and trim them so they measure 8$\frac{5}{16}$ x 9$\frac{7}{16}$ inches (21.3 x 24 cm).

2 Select a window size—either vertical or horizontal—for your photographs, and cut a window template from scrap cardstock. Trying using a set square to make sure you have 90° corners.

3 Open the folder flat, and trace the window template on the inside of the folder 1$\frac{1}{4}$ inches (3.2 cm) away from the fold. Cut out the window with a knife, using a ruler as a guide. Be careful not to cut past the corners. Repeat this for both sides of all the folders except one; save one for the back cover.

4 Open the folders, and place the photo corners on the inside of each window. Position your photographs facing out. It's easier to place them now, but you can access them via the top of each folder to change them later.

5 To make a template for the stitching, trim the scrap cardboard so it's 1$\frac{3}{16}$ x 9$\frac{7}{16}$ inches (3 x 24 cm). Mark and pierce the template with four holes evenly spaced along the center.

6 Align the template with the left edge of the folders (the open edges), and score the folder along the right edge of the template; this will make it easier to fold back the pages of the completed book. Repeat along the open edge of every folder.

7 Determine the order of your pages and stack them together with the back cover on the bottom. Secure the stack with a clip.

8 Make sure all the folded edges lie to the right. Position the template on the left side of the pages—the open sides—with the line of holes 1$\frac{3}{16}$ inches (3 cm) in from the edge, and clip it in place.

9 Use the awl to push through the marked points on your template and the pages to create holes. Wiggle the awl around to make good-sized holes; the string will lace through each hole several times.

10 Remove the template and reclip the pages together.

Assembling the Book

11 Start the Japanese stab binding with the top hole, entering from the front. Leaving 4 inches (10.2 cm) of string, loop over the top edge of the book and re-enter the same hole. Continue stitching down the spine and then work your way back up, filling in the missing stitches as illustrated (figure 1).

12 Tie off the string in a tight knot, leaving 4 inches (10 cm) and looping behind the first thread hole. Attach the beads to the tail, and finish with a knot to secure them. Press the book under heavy weights overnight.

Finished dimensions
8$\frac{3}{4}$ x 9$\frac{1}{2}$ inches (22.2 x 24.1 cm)

Materials
11 manila folders

Scrap cardstock and cardboard

80 photo corners or sticky tape

Photographs

Natural string

Beads for decoration (optional)

Tools
Basic Tool Kit (page 8)

Set square

Stitch
Japanese stab binding (page 132)

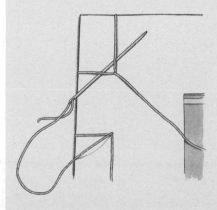

figure 1

Weatherproof Journal

Designer: Michelle Francis

With a painted weatherproof mailing envelope for the cover
and foldout packing paper pages for maps or large sketches,
this project turns simple mailing materials into a hardy journal
fit for the trail.

Creating the Cover

1 Open the weatherproof envelope at the seams. Paint the unprinted side of the envelope as desired. Allow the painted surface to dry.

2 Measure and cut the envelope into three 24-inch-long (61 cm) strips that are 5½, 4½, and 1½ inches (14, 11.4, and 3.8 cm) wide (figure 1). Save the scraps for later.

3 Measure and cut pieces of folder stock: two 4½ x 6 inches (11.4 x 15.2 cm) and one 4½ x 12¼ inches (11.4 x 31.1 cm).

4 On the unpainted side of the 5½-inch-wide (14 cm) strip, lightly score a horizontal line ½ inch (1.3 cm) in from each long edge. Fold the scored edges. With a pencil, mark the horizontal center of the strip. On either side of the center mark, slip the 4½-inch (11.4 cm) pieces of folder stock underneath the folded edges. Glue the folded edges and the spine area to the folder stock (figure 2).

TIP: As you work, smooth all your folds and glued areas with a bone folder to get rid of wrinkles and air bubbles.

---

5 Cut a 4⅜-inch (11.2 cm) square from the 4½-inch-wide (11.4 cm) painted envelope strip. Glue it to the spine area and a portion of the folder stock.

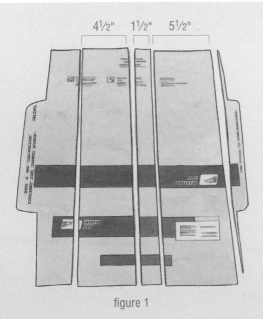

4½" 1½" 5½"

figure 1

figure 2

Finished dimensions
6 x 4½ inches (15.2 x 11.4 cm)

Materials
Newspaper

Weatherproof mail envelope, 11½ x 15 inches (29.2 x 38.1 cm) or larger

Acrylic paint in 2 or 3 colors

Scrap paper

Folder stock, two at 4½ x 6 inches (11.4 x 15.2 cm) and one 4½ x 12¼ inches (11.4 x 31.1 cm)

8 pieces white packing paper (not newsprint), 12 x 19 inches (30.5 x 48.3 cm) or larger

Template (page 139)

Two-holed vintage button

Waxed linen thread

Small scrap piece of book board

Tools
Basic Tool Kit (page 8)

Paint palette or small plate

Sponge

Small spray bottles, one for each color of acrylic paint

Small weight

Stitch
Pamphlet stitch (page 131)

6 Measure and trim the unglued ends of the cover to 5½ inches (14 cm) long, and fold them in towards the spine. Glue only the painted, folded edges to the cover. This creates a space to hold the text blocks.

Making the Text Block

7 If desired, paint your text pages. Dilute acrylic paint with water, place it in a spray bottle, and mist a sheet of packing paper. Allow each side of the paper to dry before you paint the reverse side.

8 Trim two of the sheets to 12 x 17½ inches (30.5 x 44.5 cm) to create two foldout pages. Fold and cut each sheet according to the template.

9 Measure and cut sixteen 4½ x 11¾-inch (11.4 x 30 cm) pages. Fold eight sheets together to form a signature. Insert the signature into the foldout page with the smaller foldout on the left. Repeat with the other eight sheets. Each signature should be no thicker than ⅛ inch (3 mm) at the spine. If they seem too bulky, remove one or two folios.

10 Cut a 4½-inch (11.4 cm) square from the remaining 4½-inch-wide (11.4 cm) strip of cover material. Glue the square in the center of the remaining piece of folder stock. Use a bone folder to smooth out any wrinkles and to adhere the edges.

11 Fold the strip in half with the painted envelope on the outside. Set the fold with a bone folder. With a ruler and a bone folder, score a line ⅜ inch (9.5 mm) on each side of the fold.

12 Make a punch template with three equally spaced holes for a pamphlet stitch binding. Put your awl through the middle hole to align the text block (figure 3).

figure 3

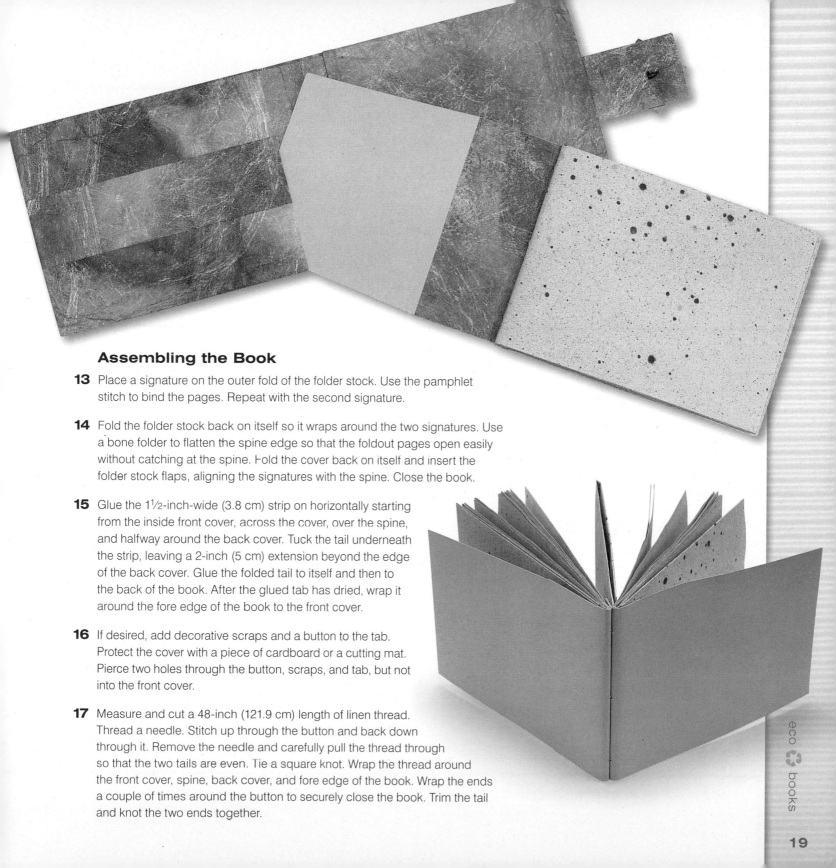

Assembling the Book

13 Place a signature on the outer fold of the folder stock. Use the pamphlet stitch to bind the pages. Repeat with the second signature.

14 Fold the folder stock back on itself so it wraps around the two signatures. Use a bone folder to flatten the spine edge so that the foldout pages open easily without catching at the spine. Fold the cover back on itself and insert the folder stock flaps, aligning the signatures with the spine. Close the book.

15 Glue the 1½-inch-wide (3.8 cm) strip on horizontally starting from the inside front cover, across the cover, over the spine, and halfway around the back cover. Tuck the tail underneath the strip, leaving a 2-inch (5 cm) extension beyond the edge of the back cover. Glue the folded tail to itself and then to the back of the book. After the glued tab has dried, wrap it around the fore edge of the book to the front cover.

16 If desired, add decorative scraps and a button to the tab. Protect the cover with a piece of cardboard or a cutting mat. Pierce two holes through the button, scraps, and tab, but not into the front cover.

17 Measure and cut a 48-inch (121.9 cm) length of linen thread. Thread a needle. Stitch up through the button and back down through it. Remove the needle and carefully pull the thread through so that the two tails are even. Tie a square knot. Wrap the thread around the front cover, spine, back cover, and fore edge of the book. Wrap the ends a couple of times around the button to securely close the book. Trim the tail and knot the two ends together.

Journey Journal

Designer: Alexia Petrakos

Created with scraps of aluminum and leather, this rustic, yet modern journal employs a stitching technique the designer learned from Suzanne Cannon of Quietfire Design.

Creating the Cover

1 Drill a set of holes near one edge of each aluminum cover. Start drilling slowly with a regular bit and don't speed up until it catches the metal. To be safe, wear a mask and goggles for this step.

2 Sand the edges and corners of the aluminum covers so they're not sharp. For a brushed aluminum look, rub each cover with fine steel wool.

3 Cut the leather so it measures $4\frac{1}{2}$ x $8\frac{3}{4}$ inches (11.4 x 22.2 cm). Copy and center the template on the leather, and use a leather punch to create the holes for the binding. Punch holes to match the ones on the aluminum covers on the edges of the leather spine.

Making the Text Block

4 Cut or tear open the paper grocery bags so they lie flat. Using a ruler or straight edge as a guide, tear 24 sheets measuring $8\frac{1}{2}$ x 11 inches (21.6 x 27.9 cm) from the grocery bags.

5 Cover one side of each sheet with gesso, letting the brown peek through in spots. Let the pages dry and then cover the other sides.

6 When the pages are dry to the touch, pile them up and place a heavy book on top to keep the edges from curling. After the gesso has dried completely, fold each sheet in half. Crease well with a bone folder.

7 Collect the paper into three signatures of eight sheets. Place each signature on your work surface with the fold to your left and mark a small dot with pencil on the upper right corner of each signature to indicate the top.

8 Fold the template in half and place it inside a signature. Make sure that the top of the template is at the head of the signature. Pierce the signature with an awl, following the guide. Repeat on the other two signatures.

Assembling the Book

9 Cut a piece of linen thread 10 times the height of the book. Run the thread through your beeswax or microcrystalline wax.

10 Thread the bookbinding needle, and lock the thread by poking the needle through the short end of the thread and pulling it down to the eye.

Finished dimensions
6 x $8\frac{3}{4}$ inches (15.2 x 22.2 cm)

Materials
Two pieces of scrap aluminum, 6 x $8\frac{3}{4}$ inches (15.2 x 22.2 cm)

Fine grit sandpaper on a wood block

Fine steel wool (optional)

Black or dark brown scrap leather

Template (page 138)

Paper grocery bags

Gesso

3 yards ($2\frac{3}{4}$ m) unwaxed red linen bookbinding thread

Beeswax or microcrystalline wax

Tools
Basic Tool Kit (page 8)

Drill with a $\frac{1}{8}$-inch (3 mm) drill bit

Mask and goggles (optional)

Leather hole punch with $\frac{1}{16}$-inch (1.6 mm) bit

Contact cement

Stitch
Harlequin stitch

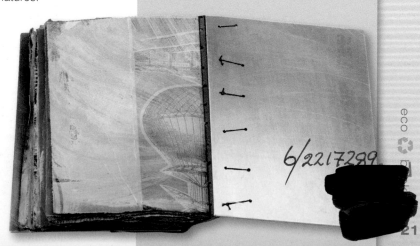

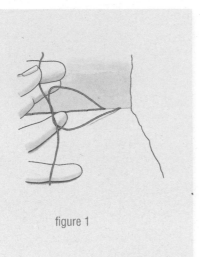

figure 1

11 Since the covers are heavy, you'll be binding the signatures directly to the leather spine before the spine is attached to the covers. Starting with the middle signature, poke the needle through the top hole on the inside and go through the middle hole at the top of the leather spine. Pull all but 4 inches (10.2 cm) of the thread through.

12 Place another signature (now called the first signature) next to the middle signature, aligning the tops. Go in the second hole down from the head through the spine into the first signature. Come back out the third hole of the first signature.

13 Insert the needle in the fourth hole down of the middle signature. Proceed going down the spine, stitching diagonally from signature to signature and alternating columns until you reach the end.

14 When you reach the bottom of the spine, go back up. Since you ended on the first column of holes in the spine, insert the needle into the first signature through the second hole from the bottom and pull through the leather spine.

15 When you've completed the X pattern up and down the first two signatures, you'll end up on the middle signature. Add the third signature at the remaining column of holes and repeat the X pattern as you did for the first two signatures.

16 When you reach the head of the middle signature for the last time, tie off the thread with a square knot and snip off the thread, leaving ¼ inch (6 mm) as illustrated (figure 1).

17 When you're done binding the signatures to the leather spine, you need to attach the spine to the covers. Rub the area around the holes in the covers with steel wool.

18 Cut and wax a 10-inch (25.4 cm) length of thread. A needle is not necessary, but if you want the extra control, thread your needle. Insert the needle from the inside of the front cover and thread it through the matching hole on the leather spine. Pull most of the thread through, leaving a couple of inches (cm) on the inside.

19 Stitch down and diagonally through the leather and the matching holes on the cover. Tie off the thread with a square knot, centering the knot in one of the cover holes. Repeat these steps to attach the back cover.

20 Adhere the corners and edges of the leather against the aluminum covers with contact cement.

Reuse Centers

Reuse centers in the United States emerged in the late 1970s and early 1980s. You're probably familiar with building-oriented reuse centers redistributing building materials either donated by local businesses or individuals or rescued from construction sites.

However, not all reuse centers are building-oriented. Creative reuse centers offer materials meant for arts and crafts. One of the oldest creative reuse centers is the East Bay Depot in Oakland, California. The East Bay Depot, like most reuse centers, is a nonprofit organization devoted to transforming ordinary materials of all kinds into whatever you can imagine.

What can you find at creative reuse centers like East Bay? A dizzying array of paper, art supplies, posters, fabric, sewing/knitting supplies, candles, foam core, fiberboard, chalk/cork boards, office and drawing supplies, CD cases, shoe boxes, film canisters, glass, tiles, carpet samples, x-rays, envelopes, trophies, toys, bric-a-brac, and ever-changing inventories.

For those who are not close to a reuse location, online centers such as Freecycle and Throwplace have developed. Users of these sites list items they would like to donate, trade, or sell for a nominal price.

Reuse centers aren't just limited to the United States. Australian nonprofit organization Reverse Garbage Truck has been operating since 1974 and was the model for the Scrap Exchange in Durham, North Carolina.

The resources listed at right are some of the larger creative reuse centers. You can also find a list of reuse centers organized by state on the REDO website (http://www.redo.org).

SOURCES

Nationwide
Freecycle (www.freecycle.org)
Throwplace (www.throwplace.com)
The Free Market (www.twincitiesfreemarket.org/)
VDumpsters (www.vdumpsters.com/)
TrashCycle (www.trashcycle.org/)

Northwest
M.E.C.C.A. (Eugene, Oregon; www.materials-exchange.org/)
S.C.R.A.P. (Portland, Oregon; www.scrapaction.org/index.html)
Cart'm (Manzanita, Oregon; http://cartm.org/)

West
The East Bay Depot for Creative Reuse (Oakland, California; www.creativereuse.org)
Scrap (San Francisco, California; www.scrap-sf.org)
FabMo (San Francisco peninsula; www.fabmo.org)
Los Angeles County Materials Exchange (LACoMax) (Los Angeles, California; www.ladpw.org/EPD/lacomax/index.cfm)
NapaMax (Napa, California; www.napamax.org/default.asp)

Midwest
Madison Stuff Exchange (Madison, Wisconsin; www.madisonstuffexchange.com)

Northeast
Creative Reuse Warehouse (Chicago, Illinois; www.resourcecenterchicago.org/crw.html)
Hudson Valley Materials Exchange (New Paltz, New York; http://hvmaterialsexchange.com)
Recycle Ann Arbor: ReUse Center (Ann Arbor, Michigan; www.recycleannarbor.org/reuse/reuse.htm)
Creative Reuse Pittsburgh (Pittsburgh, Pennsylvania; www.creativereusepgh.blogspot.com)

South
The Scrap Exchange (Durham, North Carolina; www.scrapexchange.org)
Trash 2 Treasure (Fort Lauderdale, Florida; www.trash2treasurefl.org/)
The Reusable Resources Adventure Center (Melbourne, Florida; www.reusecenterbrevard.org/)

International
Reverse Garbage Truck (Australia; www.reversegarbage.org.au/)

Photo courtesy of The Scrap Exchange, Durham, North Carolina

Cassette Tape Book

Designer: Erin Zamrzla

Got a collection of disco cassette tapes gathering dust in your closet? Turn them into mini books.

Creating the Cover

1 Clean the cassette with a moist cloth.

2 Use a ruler and pencil to draw a 4 x 2¹/₂-inch (10.2 x 6.4 cm) rectangle in the center of the book board. Flip the book board over, and draw the same size rectangle on the reverse.

3 Protect your work surface with wax paper. Use the glue and brush to apply a thin layer of glue to the book board, covering the entire area within the box that you drew. Arrange the papers you chose for your back cover within the rectangle.

4 Place a small, clean piece of wax paper over your paper, and use the flat edge of the bone paper folder to smooth the paper. This will help to remove air bubbles and excess glue.

5 Flip the back cover over onto clean wax paper. Glue the decorative papers to the inside back cover following the same steps.

6 Sandwich the back cover between clean wax paper, and press the board under a heavy stack of books or in a book press until it is dry.

7 Once dry, place the board on a cutting mat. If necessary, redraw the lines for trimming the cover. Using the metal ruler and a sharp, heavy-duty utility knife, cut out the 4 x 2¹/₂-inch (10.2 x 6.4 cm) cover. If you would like to round the corners of the cover, now is a good time to do so.

8 Place the cassette next to the back cover, face up, on a cutting mat. Use the pencil to mark the holes on the back cover, ¹/₄ inch (6 mm) in from the right edge, using the holes in the cassette as a guide as illustrated (Figure 1).

9 Use the awl to create holes in the back cover at the marks, pressing straight down through the back cover into the cutting mat.

Making the Text Block

10 Prepare the inside pages for your book by trimming the paper scraps to 3³/₄ x 4³/₄ inches (9.5 x 12 cm). Cut 61 pages.

11 Fold each page in half, smoothing the folded edges with the bone folder.

12 Nest together five folded pages (or folios) into a section. Make a total of 12 sections; you'll have one remaining folio.

Finished dimensions
2¹/₂ x 4 inches (6.4 x 10.2 cm)

Materials
Cassette tape

Book board, about 3 x 4¹/₂ inches (7.6 x 11.4 cm) and ¹/₁₆ to ¹¹/₁₆ inch (0.2 to 1.7 cm) thick

Cassette tape insert or other decorative papers for back cover

Text-weight paper scraps, to make sixty-one 3³/₄ x 4³/₄-inch (9.5 x 12 cm) pages

60 inches (152.4 cm) of 3- or 4-ply waxed linen thread

Tools
Basic Tool Kit (page 8)

Cloth

Wax paper

Stitch
Multi-needle Coptic Stitch (page 134)

figure 1

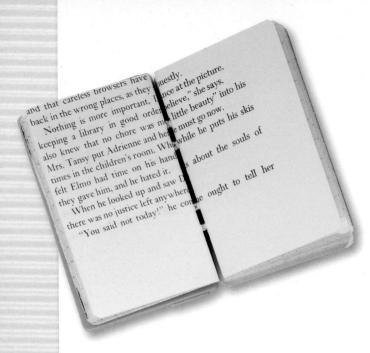

13 Create a punch template by laying the folded edge of the extra folio on top of the back cover. Line up the fold of the template along the four holes in the back cover, making sure it's centered between the top and the bottom edges. Use the pencil to mark the folded edge of the template, exactly at the holes in the back cover.

14 Open up the template and fold it so the pencil marks are on the inside of the fold. Using the template and an awl, punch straight down through the section at the four marks on the template. Repeat this for each section.

Assembling the Book

15 Stack the cassette, the text block, and the back cover, and bind the layers together using the multi-needle Coptic stitch, stitching through the holes in the cassette.

Alisa Golden
Horizon, 2007
Book, 3 x 3 x 1 inches (7.6 x 7.6 x 2.5 cm)
Found maps, linen thread, binder's board; tied binding
Photo by Sibila Savage

Carton Book

Designer: Cheryl Prose

Produce cartons are a rich source of
strong graphics. Make friends with your
grocery store's produce manager and
you'll be making dozens of colorful
(and useful) books.

Finished dimensions

5¾ x 5¼ inches (14.6 x 13.3 cm)

Materials

Cardboard box with bright colors
and bold graphics

Paper bags or craft paper

Piece of cardstock

Waxed linen thread

Tools

Basic Tool Kit (page 8)

Box cutter

Stitch

Multi-needle Coptic stitch (page 134)

Creating the Cover

1 Flatten the cardboard box, and decide which section to use for your front and back cover. With a box cutter, cut out the panels needed for the covers.

2 Place the cut cardboard pieces on your cutting mat. Using a ruler and box cutter, trim both cardboard panels to 5¾ x 5¼ inches (14.6 x 13.3 cm).

3 Cut two 1 x 5-inch (2.5 x 12.7 cm) strips out of the remaining box to use as reinforcements on the spine edge of the covers.

4 Place both covers face down on your work surface. Glue one strip of cardboard to the inside right edge of the front cover so it's flush with the spine edge and centered top to bottom. Do the same for the back cover, placing the strip on the inside left edge of the cover so it's flush with the spine edge and centered top to bottom. Place both covers under weights until the glue dries.

Making the Text Block

5 From the paper bags or craft paper, cut 27 pieces of paper to 5⅛ x 11 inches (13 x 27.9 cm).

6 Fold each piece of paper in half lengthwise. Each folded sheet will measure 5⅛ X 5½ inches (13 x 14 cm).

7 Nest three sheets of folded paper together to create nine signatures, and set the creases with a bone folder. In pencil, lightly number the signatures to help you keep them oriented correctly. Set the signature stacks aside.

8 Place the front cover face down on your work surface. Draw a line ½-inch (1.3 cm) in from the right side. Starting at the top, mark four holes along the pencil line at 1-inch (2.5 cm) increments, and punch the holes with an awl. Erase the pencil line.

9 Place the hole-punched cover face up on top of the inside back cover. Use the holes in the front cover as a template to mark the holes for the back cover. Punch the four holes in the back cover.

10 Make a punch guide for your signatures by cutting a piece of cardstock to 2½ x 5⅛ inches (6.4 x 13 cm) and fold it in half lengthwise. Place the folded edge of the template along the line of punched holes on the front cover, and mark the hole locations on the template as illustrated, including a mark at the top right corner (figure 1).

11 Using an awl and your template, punch holes in each signature.

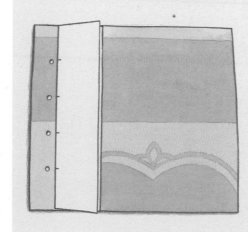

figure 1

Assembling the Book

12 Cut two pieces of waxed linen thread 44 inches (111.8 cm) long. Thread a needle onto each end of both pieces of thread.

13 Bind the book using the multi-needle Coptic stitch.

14 When you've completed the stitching, bring the threads back inside the holes in the final signature. Remove the needles, and tie off and cut the threads. Erase the numbers on the signatures.

Six-Pack Book

Designer: Michael A. Henninger

Look no further than your recycling bin for the
supplies for this accordion book, made with
two very durable beer can covers.

Creating the Cover

1 Wash the empty cans with soap and water, and let them dry. Cut off the top and the bottom of the can(s) using a utility knife and scissors. Be careful because the cut edges of the can are very sharp.

2 Cut the resulting tube lengthwise with scissors, and unroll it to make a flat sheet of aluminum. You may have to hold the piece flat because the sides will try to curl up.

3 Using a ruler and the utility knife, trim the edges straight and create a rectangle. Draw the knife multiple times to cut evenly and safely through the aluminum sheet.

4 Lightly sand the inner surface of the sheet with sand paper. Rinse the piece with water and let it dry.

5 Decide on the dimensions for your book cover based on the size of your aluminum sheet, keeping in mind that a larger can allows for a bigger book. If you are using one can, and thus have only a single sheet of aluminum, your book will be smaller because you will need to cut two pieces from the sheet (one for the front cover and one for the back). Just make sure you end up with two same-sized pieces of aluminum to create the covers.

6 Now that you have determined the dimensions for your covers, use a permanent marker to mark the dimensions on the sheet. Then use your ruler and utility knife (or scissors) to cut the two rectangles.

7 Cut two pieces of board (either binder's board or heavyweight illustration board) that measure 1 inch (2.5 cm) less than the width and height of your aluminum pieces.

8 Using your permanent marker and ruler, mark ½-inch (1.3 cm) margins on the inside surface of each aluminum piece. These will become the flaps that fold over the board's edges.

9 Brush glue (PVA or white glue) onto one surface of the board, and stick the board down onto the marked area of the aluminum. Place the cover between sheets of waxed paper and apply a bit of pressure—using a book press, weights, or a stack of books—until the glue can thoroughly dry (usually four or more hours). Repeat for the other piece of board and aluminum.

10 After the covers have dried, place the aluminum side face down. Cut off each corner of the aluminum with scissors to make a flap. Do this for all the corners of each cover.

Finished dimensions
3 x 4½ inches (7.6 x 11.4 cm)

Materials
One or two aluminum cans

Binder's board or heavyweight illustration board, about ⅒ inch (3 mm) thick

Medium weight paper, 22 inches (55.9 cm) long

Tools
Basic Tool Kit (page 8)

Sand paper (100 grit or finer)

Fine-point permanent marker

Wax paper

eco books

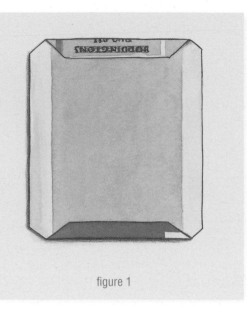

figure 1

11 Brush glue on the top flap, and then fold the flap over to glue it to the back of the board as illustrated (figure 1). Try lifting the opposite edge of the board while keeping the flap on the table or use a bone folder to fold the flap more evenly. Repeat this step for the bottom flap, applying pressure so the glue sets well (about an hour), and then do the same for the left and right sides.

Making the Text Block

12 Cut a strip of paper that will become the accordion folded page. Plan on a page size that is ¼ inch (6 mm) less than the width and length of your covers. Multiply the number of pages you'd like by the width of each page to determine the dimensions to cut your paper.

13 Accordion-fold the strip of paper into the appropriate size pages.

Assembling the Book

14 Brush glue onto the back of page one and attach it to the front cover, making sure it's right side up. Repeat this to attach the back cover. Place waxed paper between the first and last page spreads, close the book, and place it under pressure until glue dries.

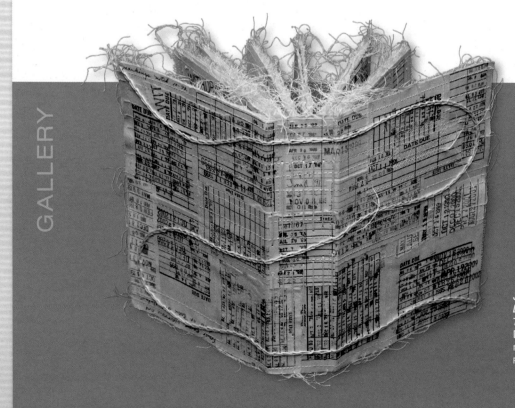

Jody Alexander
Date Due: It's Not a Popularity Contest, 2008
7¼ x 5¼ x 1¾ inches (18.4 x 13.3 x 4.4 cm)
Date due pockets from withdrawn library books, mull, thread; decorative long stitch binding
Photo by R. R. Jones

Slinky Map Book

Designer: Michelle Francis

From its flexible, toy-like form to its handy slide box container,
this project is pure fun; it's constructed entirely of old maps
using a custom stitch the designer learned from Amanda Love.

Finished dimensions

2 inches (5 cm) square

Materials

Scrap piece of cardstock, 2 x 3 inches
(5 x 7.6 cm)

Template (page 139)

3 scrap pieces of book board: 4 x 5
inches (10.2 x 12.7 cm), 4 x ½ inch
(10.2 x 1.3 cm), 4½ x ½ inch
(11.4 x 1.3 cm)

2 or 3 old highway maps

2 lengths of lightweight unwaxed linen
thread, 9 feet (2.7 m)

Beeswax

Plastic box for holding photographic
slides: approximately 3¼ x 2¼ x 2⅛
inches (8.2 x 5.7 x 5.3 cm)

Double-sided tape

Tools

Basic Tool Kit (page 8)

Making the Text Block

1 Copy the template to create a hole-punching guide for the pages, and use scrap book board and glue to create a punching jig (figure 1).

2 Cut the maps into 120 pieces, each 2 x 4 inches (5 x 10.2 cm). When the pieces are folded in half, the text should read horizontally. Save two or three pieces for the last step.

3 Create 2 x 2-inch (5 x 5 cm) folios by folding the pieces of paper in half, remembering that the inside of the folio will show more than the outside in the finished book. Use a bone folder to crease the folds, and then choose two folios to be your first and last pages.

4 Use the template and awl to punch holes into the right-hand side of your first folio and the left-hand side of your last folio. Arrange the remaining folios in several stacks. Use small weights to hold the stacks in place.

5 Punch holes in the folded folio stacks—three or four folios at a time—using the template as a guide and making sure the holes are ¼ inch (6 mm) from the spine (as they are on the template). Make sure the folded edges are together and that the holes from one folio line up with the holes in the next folio. Take your time squaring up the folded pages in the jig, and keep the punched folios neatly stacked (figure 1).

Assembling the Book

6 Run your thread through beeswax. Thread a needle (four total) onto each end of both lengths of thread.

7 Begin by punching your needles halfway through the holes in your first folio—on the right-hand side—and into the holes on the left-hand side of the next folio. Make sure the threads don't become entwined by keeping them parallel and even in length. Carefully pull the needles through the holes, two at a time.

TIP: To avoid tangles, keep the two left-hand needles to the left side and the two right-hand needles to the right side as best you can.

8 Keep the spine of the book parallel to you; take the next opened folio and place it back to back with your second folio.

9 Take needle one (far left-hand needle) and put it into hole number two. Pull it through, coming out of hole two in folio three. Take needle two through hole number one, coming out of hole one in the center of folio three. You will have created an X. Repeat with needles three and four. You will have two Xs in the center of folio two (figure 2).

10 Close folio one and two and tug gently to snug up the threads. The Xs will give the pages tension and allow the book to have a springy quality. The Xs will only appear in the centers of each folio—not between the folios—and the thread shouldn't be visible when looking at the spine. Repeat steps eight through 10 with additional folios, remembering to snug up the thread before adding another folio.

TIP: Loops on the spine indicate that the thread wasn't properly snugged. Occasionally check the spine to make sure this isn't happening.

---

11 After 75 pages, check how your book fits into the slide box, adding more folios if necessary. The thickness of the thread and the paper you're using will affect the number of folios you'll need. The book should fit snugly, but not so tightly that you damage the pages getting the book in and out of the box.

12 Add your last folio. After pulling the thread through, remove the needles and snug up the thread. Tie a square knot using threads one and two, and tie another square knot using threads three and four (figure 3). Finish by trimming the ends to about ½ inch (1.3 cm).

Creating the Cover

13 From the pieces you set aside in step 2, pick one for the top of the box cover and one for the inside. Trim the pieces to size and adhere them using double-sided tape. Attach a third piece to the outside bottom of the box if you like.

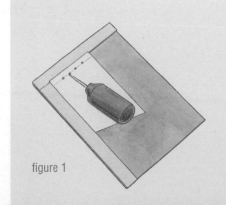

figure 1

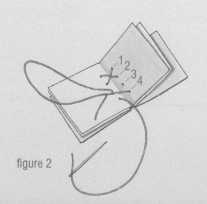

figure 2

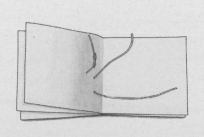

figure 3

Dos-a-Dos

Designer: Cheryl Prose

Got a stack of old gift cards or credit
cards lying around? Put them to
good use—again—as covers for a
handy dos-a-dos book, perfect for
quick notes and lists.

Making the Text Block

1 Fold each piece of text-weight paper in half to create folded sheets that measure 2^1/$_{16}$ x 3^1/$_4$ inches (5.2 x 8.3 cm).

2 Trim the top and bottom corner of the folded edge of each signature with a corner rounder.

3 Nest four sheets of folded paper together to create 14 signatures. Run a bone folder along the folded edge of each signature to set the crease.

4 Make two stacks of seven signatures with the folded edges to the left side. In pencil, lightly number the signatures, and set the signature stacks aside.

Creating the Cover

5 Place the cover card face up on your work surface. In pencil, draw a vertical line ^{3}/$_8$ inch (9.5 mm) in from the left side of the card.

6 Starting at the top, mark two holes along the pencil line at ^{1}/$_2$ and 1^1/$_2$ inches (1.3 and 3.8 cm). Punch the two marked holes with the hole punch and erase the pencil line.

7 Stack the punched card on top of the back cover card with both facing up. Use the holes in the first card as a template to mark and punch the holes for the card below. Repeat this step on the left and right side of the center card; your center cover card should now have four holes, two at each end.

8 To create a punch template for your text block, fold your piece of cardstock in half. Place the folded edge of the template along the line of punched holes on one of the cards. Mark where each hole falls on the template. Reverse the fold of the template, and use an awl to punch the two holes marked on the template. Punch holes in all the signatures, and restack them in order.

Finished dimensions:
3^3/$_8$ x 2^1/$_8$ inches (8.6 x 5.4 cm)

Materials
56 pieces of text-weight paper, cut to 2^1/$_{16}$ x 6^1/$_2$ inches (5.2 x 16.5 cm)

Three redeemed gift cards or promotional credit cards

2^1/$_{16}$-inch square (5.2 cm) piece of cardstock

Two pieces of waxed linen thread, each 36 inches (91.4 cm) long

Tools
Basic Tool Kit (page 8)

^{1}/$_4$-inch (6 mm) hole punch

Stitch
Multi-needle Coptic stitch (page 134)

Assembling the Book

9 Thread a needle onto each end of one piece of waxed linen thread.

10 Beginning in signature one, take the thread through both holes with one needle going through each hole. Even up the threads.

11 Place the card you have chosen for the front cover on top of the first signature with the front of the card facing out.

12 Loop the needles around the outside of the card and through the corresponding hole, keeping the needles to the inside of the pair of holes. Tighten the threads.

13 Take the needles back into their respective hole in signature one. Add the rest of the signatures in the first set using the multi-needle Coptic stitch, dropping down below the previous signature each time for the chain stitch.

14 When the first set of signatures is sewn in place, place the center cover on top of the sewn signatures. The front of the center cover card can face either direction as long as the tops of the cards are aligned. Loop the needles through the corresponding holes on the center cover, going from the outside of the cover to the space between the cover and final signature. Keep the needle to the inside of the pair of holes, and tighten the threads.

15 Drop down below the seventh signature and chain stitch. Bring the threads back inside the holes in the seventh signature. Remove the needles, and tie off and cut the threads. Erase the numbers on the signatures.

16 Thread a needle on each end of the second piece of waxed linen thread.

17 Attach the next set of signatures following the same steps you followed to attach the first set.

18 When the second set of signatures is sewn in place, add the back cover following the steps you used to add the front cover.

Jewel Case

Designer: Donna J. Engstrom

This project turns an everyday office
supply—a CD case—into a gold-
toned container for a disc-sized
accordion fold book.

Finished dimensions

6 x 5 inches (15.2 x 12.7 cm)

Materials

Old CD with jewel case

Silver spray paint

6-inch (15.2 cm) square piece of mat board

Gold and black acrylic paint

Scraps of patterned tissue paper

Matte medium

Tiny twigs

Small wood beads

6 x 30-inch (15.2 x 76.2 cm) strip of lightweight printmaking paper

Tools

Basic Tool Kit (page 8)

Medium-grit sandpaper

Newspaper

Paint palette

Spray bottle with water

Masking tape

Creating the Cover

1 Lightly sand the entire CD case to make sure the paint will stick. Wipe off the dust, and lay the case on newspaper.

2 Spray the case with silver paint, allowing each side to dry before turning it over. Allow the case to dry a few hours before going to the next step.

3 Measure and cut the mat board to fit inside the front cover and cut a 1-inch-wide (2.5 cm) strip the length of front cover.

4 Pour a small amount of the gold and black paint onto a palette. Using a brush and water, mix a tiny bit of black with the gold to darken it. Continue thinning the paint until you have a soupy consistency.

5 Paint one side of the case quickly; it doesn't need to be neat.

6 Before the paint dries, hold the spray bottle about 12 inches (30.5 cm) from the case's surface, and spray lightly. If you use too much water, you will lose the effect. Repeat this process for the other side of the case and for the mat board pieces.

7 Slide the dry, painted mat board into the inside front cover, making sure it fits snugly; glue the pieces in place if desired.

8 Add design elements with strips of masking tape to the inside and outside of the case. Paint the tape with the gold and black mixture.

9 Once the paint has dried, tear strips of patterned tissue, and glue them in place with matte medium.

10 Glue the 1-inch (2.5 cm) strip of mat board onto the cover.

11 Once everything is dry and in place, give the entire case a protective coating using matte medium. Let the case dry overnight.

12 Break your sticks into roughly 2- to 2½-inch-long (5 to 6.4 cm) pieces. Slip the pieces into beads, and glue them in place. Set the case aside to dry.

Making the Text Block

13 Accordion-fold the 30-inch-long (76.2 cm) strip of paper, using the CD as a template as illustrated (figure 1).

14 Place the CD on top of the paper, and lightly trace around it with a pencil.

15 Using scissors, trim the pages following your traced line, leaving a section of the folded pages uncut. This is very important or the pages will no longer be connected.

16 Paint or decorate the pages as desired.

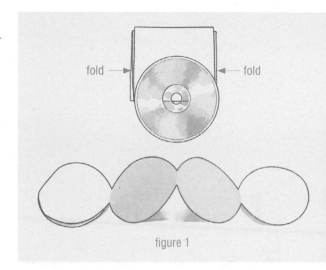

fold → ← fold

figure 1

Charlene Asato
Feathers Found, 2006
5 x 9 x 5 inches (12.7 x 22.9 x 12.7 cm)
Scrap lumber, used screws and nails, packaging plastic sleeves packing paper, product strapping tape; sewn
Photo by artist

Taller Leñateros:
The Woodlanders' Workshop

Founded in 1975 by Mexican poet Ambar Past, Taller Leñateros, which translates to The Woodlanders' Workshop, is the only publishing house in Mexico run by Mayan artists. Located in the Mayan Highland of southern Mexico, in San Cristobal de las Casas, Chiapas, we transform what others throw away into beautiful books.

Among our many objectives, Taller Leñateros promotes the documentation, praise, and dissemination of Amerindian and popular cultural values: song, literature, the arts, and the revitalization of old and endangered techniques such as the extraction of dyes from wild plants. We cultivate a group environment in which all the members of the workshop participate in decisions and solutions in order to benefit the individual and the group. Although we are not all from the same culture and we speak different languages, we are working together for a common project.

We benefit the ecology by recycling agricultural and industrial wastes to create the covers, endpapers, and wrappings for our books, and we generate worthwhile and decently paid employment for the women and men in our community. Taller Leñateros is also a multi-ethnic space for established and rising artists. We foment artistic creation among the most marginalized communities, and we invent, teach, and practice the arts of handmade paper, bookbinding, solar silkscreen, painting, woodcuts, and natural dyes.

In our backyard, big kettles are boiling full of corn husks, gladiola stems, palm leaves, recycled women's blouses, old cardboard boxes, and many other raw materials to make paper. We beat the natural fibers for our paper in a mill that spins by bicycle power.

Our handmade books and artwork are the products of many found materials. We collect withered flowers from churches, pine needles from festivals, banana leaves (the banana tree produces fruit once and then dies), heart of the maguey plant (which we find as refuse from the tequila industry), corn husks, bridal veil plants, bean pods, reeds, coconut shells, carnation stems, palm fronds, grass, papyrus, cattails, and bamboo as well as recycled cardboard boxes and old clothes. The raw material of dreams is nearly always something considered useless.

Little by little, without subsidies or capitalist partners, we have been able to buy and construct the minimal equipment with which we work. Using scavenged and recycled materials, we have managed to construct our workshop with our own hands. The only resource we have had, and the most valuable resource we maintain, is ourselves: our collective ideas and our creativity.

We recycle our visions to turn them into art.

OPPOSITE: The cover of this book, entitled *Bolom Chon*, is made of recycled cardboard boxes, the endpapers are made from maguey fiber (a waste product of the tequila industry), and the text—an ancient Mayan song about a jaguar in the rain forest—is printed on recycled paper.

TOP: Mayan paper makers show off mask covers made from recycled cardboard boxes.

LEFT: The bicycle-powered paper mill in action.

BELOW LEFT: In the center's backyard, paper is made of recycled agricultural and industrial waste.

Baggage Tag Book

Designer: Erin Zamrzla

With a colorful tag cover, this simple pamphlet stitch booklet
creates the perfect memento of a recent journey or a handy
spot for new travel notes.

Creating the Cover

1 Score the center of the tag parallel to the short side. Fold the tag in half along the score. Once folded, the top and bottom of the tag become the fore edges of the cover and the fold becomes the spine.

Making the Text Block

2 Measure the size of the tag. Cut the text pages so that they are ¼ inch (6 mm) smaller than the height of your tag and ½ inch (1.3 cm) smaller than the length.

3 Fold each page in half. Use the bone paper folder to smooth each fold.

4 Open up one folded page and place the ruler along the center fold. Make three pencil marks along the fold: at the very center, ¼-inch (6 mm) from the top of the page, and ¼-inch (6 mm) from the bottom of the page. This page will serve as the punch template.

Assembling the Book

5 Nest all 16 folios (folded pages) together, making sure that the template is on the top and that the pencil marks are visible. Pierce the holes with the awl, using the template as a guide.

TIP: If you'd like to round the corners of the pages, first secure the pages together with a clip.

---

6 Lay the cover flat with the template page on top and use the awl to punch the three holes.

7 Place all of the folded pages in the cover, aligning the pierced holes.

8 Thread a needle with a single length of waxed linen. Pull a few inches (cm) through the eye of the needle.

TIP: Flatten one end of the waxed linen by scraping your fingernail along the end. This will help you insert it into the eye of a needle.

---

9 Sew the pages to the cover using a three-hole pamphlet stitch. Knot the thread with a square knot when you finish sewing.

10 If the tag has an elastic band through its hole, use the band as a closure for the finished book.

Finished dimensions
2⅜ x 2 inches (6.1 x 5.1 cm)

Materials
Baggage tag

Text-weight paper

3- or 4-ply waxed linen thread

Tools
Basic Tool Kit (page 8)

Stitch
Three-hole pamphlet stitch (page 131)

Fold-a-Book

Designer: Geri Michelli

Based on a design by Shereen LaPlantz,
the text block is super-simple to construct
using a sheet of paper, a recycled grocery
bag, or newsprint.

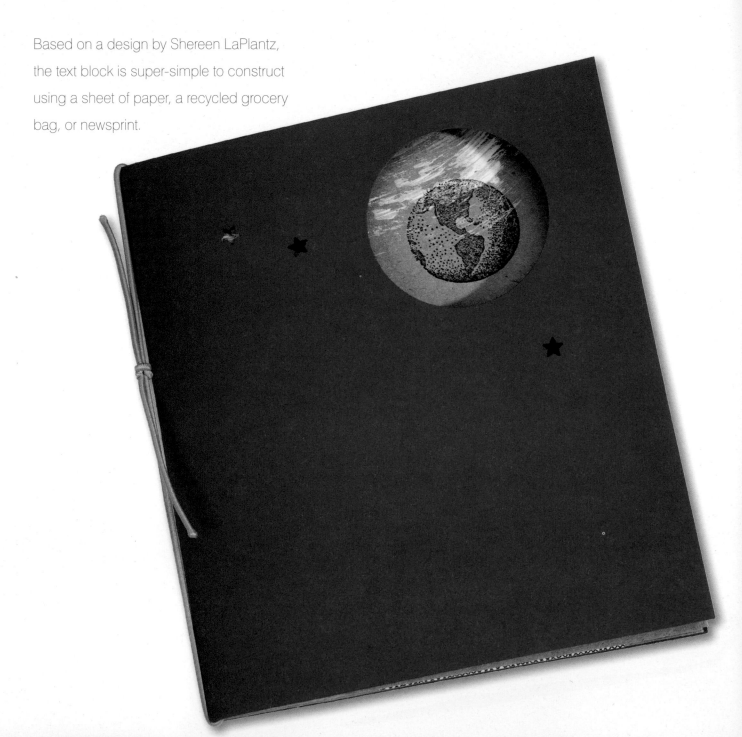

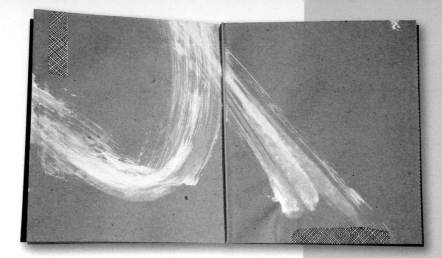

Making the Text Block

1 Randomly paint broad brush strokes in white acrylic on the paper. Once the paint has dried, iron the paper from the back to flatten it.

2 Fold the paper in half lengthwise with the painted side out. Open it up, then fold it in quarters crosswise.

3 Cut along the center fold line, across the center two quarters (figure 1). Fold the paper lengthwise so the cut is at the top.

4 Push the ends together to form a diamond-shaped opening at the top (figure 2). Keep pushing to close the diamond shape.

5 Two of the pages will have openings at the fore edge (figure 3). Seal them by pasting scraps of business envelopes—pattern side out—over the edges.

Creating the Cover

6 Cut the cardstock to 11 x 6¼ inches (27.9 x 15.9 cm), and fold it in half.

7 Attach the cover to the pages with elastic cord. Embellish the cover with punches.

Finished dimensions
5½ x 6¼ inches (14 x 15.9 cm)

Materials
Gesso or white acrylic paint

Brown wrapping paper from a newspaper or recycled paper, about 21½ x 12½ inches (54.6 x 31.8 cm)

Recycled security envelopes, with a pattern on the inside

Cardstock for cover

14 inches (35.6 cm) of elastic cord

Tools
Basic Tool Kit (page 8)

Decorative paper punches

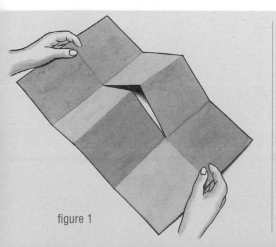

figure 1

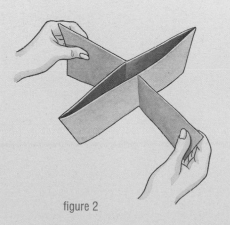

figure 2

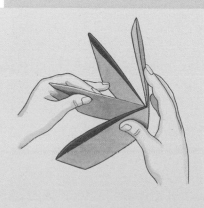

figure 3

Book Preserves

Designer: Cassie Ogle

This project puts an artistic spin on preservation: books made from old encyclopedia pages are displayed in an antique canning jar.

Making the Text Block

1 Carefully cut pages from the encyclopedia using a utility knife and a ruler.

2 Fold each page in half widthwise. Use a bone folder to make a crisp fold, and then slide the bone folder through the crease to cut the paper apart.

3 Fold and cut the two page halves in half again widthwise.

4 Fold and cut the four page quarters in half again to create eight sections which measure approximately 4 x 2¾ inches (10.2 x 7 cm).

5 Stack the cut sheets into sets of four, and fold each stack in half to create a signature. Repeat until you have 15 signatures.

6 Using a ruler, pencil, and piece of cardboard or cardstock, create a template with marks for the top and bottom edge of the book spine. Measuring from the top edge mark, make additional marks at ¼ inch, ⅞ inch, 1⅝ inch, and 2¼ inches (.6, 2.2, 4.1, 5.7 cm).

7 Align the text block so that the top of the spine aligns with the top mark on the template. Using the template and a triangle to make straight lines, mark the signatures.

8 Use the awl to punch a hole at each mark on the signature. Repeat for each signature.

Assembling the Book

9 Cut two lengths of sewing thread approximately 35 inches (88.9 cm) long. Pull them through wax until they are lightly coated. Thread each end onto a needle (4 needles total).

10 Stitch the pages together using the multi-needle Coptic stitch.

11 Tie off the threads using square knots, and cut the excess thread.

12 Repeat to make enough books to fill your jar.

Finished dimensions
2 x 2¾ inches (5 x 7 cm) each

Materials
Encyclopedia

Cardboard or cardstock

Sewing thread

Wax

Large glass jar

Tools
Basic Tool Kit (page 8)

Stitch
Multi-needle Coptic Stitch (page 134)

Faux Leather Journal

Designer: Heather Crossley

Once coated with shellac, this delicate but striking cover—
pieced together from used tea bags—takes on an aged,
leather-like appearance.

Creating the Cover

1 Using a sewing machine and black thread, sew a pieced double layer of teabags together using a zigzag stitch.

2 Continue piecing the teabags together until you've created a large rectangular piece that measures $12\frac{3}{4}$ x $8\frac{1}{2}$ inches (32 x 21.6 cm), or the desired size for your cover. Make sure to stitch down all the areas where the teabags overlap, but don't worry about knotting the thread ends.

3 Working in a well-ventilated area, coat the piece with a generous amount of shellac. Hang the piece up loosely and allow it to dry thoroughly.

Making the Text Block

4 Fold your tan pages in half and nest them together to create five signatures of four pages each.

5 Make a punch template by folding a piece of scrap paper in half and aligning the fold with the fold of one of the signatures. Mark as many evenly spaced holes as desired on the template. Use the awl, a phone book for a cradle, and the template to punch holes in the center fold of all the signatures.

Assembling the Book

6 Use the template as a guide to punch holes in the cover.

7 Reinforce the punch holes by inserting eyelets, reinforced with a small piece of brown handmade paper, in the holes.

8 Bind the cover to the signatures using the multi-needle Coptic stitch, with an exposed stitch binding.

Finished dimensions:
$6\frac{1}{2}$ x $8\frac{1}{2}$ inches (16.5 x 21.6 cm)

Materials

Black thread

24 used teabags

Shellac

20 sheets of tan paper

Piece of scrap paper

Tan linen thread

Black eyelets

4 small rectangular pieces of brown handmade paper

Tools

Basic Tool Kit (page 8)

Sewing machine

Stitch

Multi-needle Coptic stitch (page 134) with exposed stitch binding

MAKE YOUR OWN SHELLAC

In a glass jar, mix one part shellac flakes to three parts methylated spirit, and let the mixture dissolve. The longer you leave it, the darker the mixture will become. If the mixture becomes too thick, add more methylated spirit. Use a dedicated brush to apply the mixture to the teabags. The brush can only be cleaned with methylated spirit. Do not use water; it will harden the bristles.

Hard Pack Book

Designer: Mauro Toledo

Make the most of a bad habit by converting
a cigarette box into a mini journal that fits
perfectly in your pocket.

Creating the Cover

1 Cut the cigarette box open by cutting, with scissors, through the center of one long and both short sides. Open the box and lay it out flat, face up. Tape the opening flap to the front lower panel so it remains closed.

2 Cut two 6- to 7-inch (15.2 to 17.8 cm) strips of packing tape. Place one over the top half of the cigarette box and the other over the bottom half. Abut the edges of the tape, although some overlap is okay.

3 Use your utility knife to trim away the edges, leaving only the front cover, spine, and back cover sections.

4 Glue cardstock to the inside of the box. On top of the cardstock, glue artwork, patterned paper, or photography. Cover the box with wax paper, and place it under a few heavy books while it dries.

5 Once dry, trim off the extra cardstock and paper edges. Score lines along the inside of the cover to create the spine, and fold along the scores.

Making the Text Block

6 From each sheet of 8½ x 11-inch (21.6 x 27.9cm) paper, cut six 4 x 3⅛-inch (10.2 x 7.9 cm) pieces. This should give you 66 sheets, two of which you will not need.

7 Fold the pages in half widthwise. Arrange the pages into stacks of eight, creating eight signatures.

Assembling the Book

8 Trim a piece of graph paper so it's the same size as the spine. Draw a binding design on the paper, and use it as a punch template for the spine.

9 Fold the towel in half twice to protect your work surface. Use the awl to punch holes through the spine, work gently so the holes don't become stretched out.

10 Center each signature vertically in the cover. Use a pencil to mark where you want the hole in the signature so that it lines up with the holes in the spine and sits centered in the cover. Punch holes in all the signatures at the marks.

11 Bind the book using long stitch.

Finished dimensions
2⅛ x 3¼ inches (5.3 x 8.3 cm)

Materials
Empty cigarette box, 2⅛ x 3¼ inches (5.3 x 8.3 cm)

Clear packing tape

Cardstock

Piece of patterned paper or artwork

11 pieces of paper, 8½ x 11 inches (21.6 x 27.9 cm)

Piece of graph paper

28 inches (71.1 cm) of hemp or linen binding thread

Tools
Basic Tool Kit (page 8)

Stitch
Long stitch (page 132)

Coffee Codex

Designer: Karen J. Lauseng

One part book and one part
sculpture, this project uses a
number of recycled and found
materials from used coffee filters
to bamboo skewers.

Making the Text Block

1 Flatten the used filters and let them dry completely, with the grounds still in them. By experimenting with the placement of the grounds, you can achieve a variety of patterns.

2 Use a firm brush—such as a shaving, stencil, or paint brush—to remove the grounds from the filters. Collect and prepare 45 used coffee filters.

TIP: Using different kinds of coffee will create different colors and textures for the pages. Organic coffee produces dark, dense patterns while milder roasts create softer shades of brown.

---

3 Set your iron to the dry cotton setting, and place a protective cloth on the ironing board. Place a moist pressing cloth between the iron and the filter and press to remove any wrinkles. Fold the filter in half, and press a crease down the center. Arrange the coffee filters in 15 signatures of three.

4 To make a template for notching the coffee filters, position a pressed coffee filter on top of a folded piece of cardstock, aligning both fold lines. Trace around the outer edge of the filter, and cut out the half circle to form the shape of your template.

5 Measure ½ inch (1.3 cm) from the fold line of the template, and draw a line. Measuring from the top, mark five points along the line you just drew; the first mark should be 1½ inches (3.8 cm) from the top, followed by four marks at 1¼-inch (3.2 cm) intervals. Then cut a ⅛-inch (3 mm) notch in the template at each mark.

6 Place a signature inside the template, and cut slits in the filters matching the notches in the template (figure 1). Repeat the process with each signature.

Finished dimensions
8 x 14 inches (20.3 x 35.6 cm)

Materials
46 used coffee filters

Cardstock

15 bamboo skewers, 11¾ inches (30 cm) tall with similar diameters

Old wooden candleholder

½ yard (0.5 m) of waxed linen thread

Tools
Basic Tool Kit (page 8)

Iron

Pressing cloth

Candle

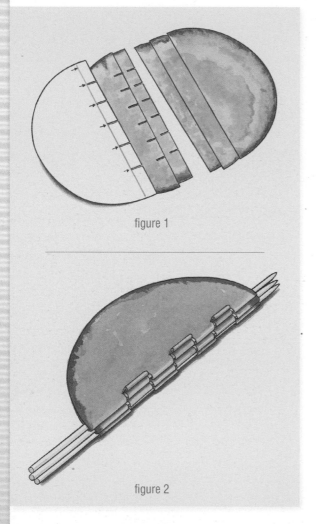

figure 1

figure 2

Assembling the Book

7 Use a candle to singe the tip of each bamboo skewer just enough to darken it. For safety reasons, do this outside or in a well-ventilated area, and keep a cup of water nearby.

TIP: Candleholders have various depths so you may need to adjust the length of the bamboo skewers. To test for size, insert a skewer into the center hole of the candleholder. The length should measure between 8¾ and 9 inches (22.2 to 22.9 cm) from the upper edge of the candleholder to the tip of the bamboo skewer. If necessary, use a utility knife to shorten the skewers before weaving.

---

8 Weave a bamboo skewer through the center of the first signature. Alternate the weave pattern—skipping every other loop as you work—and connect each successive signature by weaving through the loops you skipped with the previous skewer (figure 2). When you get to the end, connect the last signature to the first signature to form a circle.

10 Place white glue inside the center hole of the candleholder and on the blunt ends of the bamboo skewers. Insert the bamboo skewers into the hole.

11 While the glue is still wet, cut a ½-yard (0.5 m) piece of waxed linen thread, and weave it in and out through the tips of the bamboo skewers. Pull the thread tight while maintaining the integrity of the circle of bamboo skewers. Add a touch of white glue to the ends of the thread to hold it in place. When the glue is dry, clip the thread.

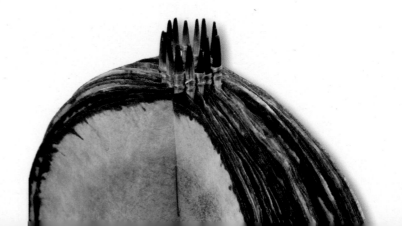

Diskette Book

Designer: Cheryl Prose

Diskettes may be a thing of the past, but this
project is very progressive. Its inventive covers
make other books seem old-fashioned.

Finished dimensions

3$\frac{1}{2}$ inches (8.9 cm) square

Materials

Two 3$\frac{1}{2}$-inch (8.9 cm) computer diskettes

36 pieces of text-weight paper

3$\frac{1}{2}$-inch (8.9 cm) square of cardstock

2 pieces of waxed linen thread, 36 inches (152.4 cm) each

Tools

Basic Tool Kit (page 8)

$\frac{1}{4}$-inch (6 mm) hole punch or drill with a $\frac{1}{4}$-inch (6 mm) bit

Stitch

Multi-needle Coptic stitch (page 134)

Creating the Cover

1 Place one computer diskette on your work surface with the round metal hub facing up. With a pencil, draw a vertical line $\frac{1}{4}$ inch (6 mm) in from the left side of the disk.

2 Mark four holes from the top edge, along the pencil line at $\frac{3}{4}$, 1$\frac{1}{4}$, 2$\frac{1}{4}$, and 3 inches (1.9, 3.2, 5.7, and 7.6 cm). Punch or drill holes at the four markings. Erase the pencil line.

3 Stack the punched diskette on top of the second diskette with both disks facing the same direction so they line up exactly. Use the holes in the first disk as a template to mark the holes for the disk below. Punch or drill the four holes in the second disk.

Making the Text Block

4 Cut the text-weight paper into 36 pieces, each 3$\frac{1}{2}$ x 6$\frac{11}{16}$ inches (8.9 x 14.2 cm). Fold each piece in half. Each folded sheet will measure 3$\frac{1}{2}$ x 3$\frac{5}{16}$ inches (8.9 x 8.8 cm).

5 Nest four sheets of folded paper together to create nine signatures. Run a bone folder along the folded edge of each signature to set the crease.

6 Stack the signatures one on top of the other with the folded edges to the left side. In pencil, lightly number the signatures at the top right-hand corner.

7 To create the punch template for your signature, fold the 3$\frac{1}{2}$-inch (8.9 cm) square of cardstock in half. Place the folded edge of the template along the line of punched holes on one of the diskettes. Center the template top to bottom; mark the holes and mark the top right corner on the template. Reverse the fold of the template so that the marks are inside.

8 Use an awl and the template to punch holes in each signature. Restack them in order.

Assembling the Book

9 Thread a needle on each end of both pieces of waxed linen thread.

10 Place the diskette you have chosen for the front cover on top of the first signature with the round metal hub facing out and the metal shutter at the top.

11 Beginning inside the first signature, take one thread through sewing stations one and two. Take the second thread through sewing stations three and four. Even up the threads.

12 Loop the needles around the outside of the diskette and through the corresponding holes, keeping the needles to the interior of each pair of holes as illustrated (figure 1). Tighten the threads.

13 Take the needles back into their respective hole in the first signature. Continue sewing the signatures in place using the multi-needle Coptic stitch. Attach the back cover with the same process that you used for the front cover.

14 Tie off and cut the threads. Erase the numbers on the signatures.

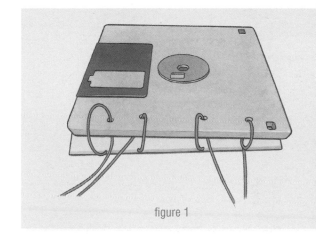

figure 1

Ashlee Weitlauf
16th Street & Highland Avenue, 2002
3¹⁵⁄₁₆ x 3⁵⁄₁₆ x 1¹⁵⁄₁₆ inches (10 x 8.5 x 5 cm)
Wooden boards from the gables of a house that was illegally demolished, handmade paper; Coptic bound, letterpress printing
Photo by artist

Margaret Couch Cogswell
There Are Days..., 2007
3½ x 2½ x 2½ inches (8.9 x 6.4 x 6.4 cm)
Tin can top, champagne cage, old buttons, wire, bottle cap, milk paint, spray paint, recycled shirt board, paper, thread, graphite; accordion fold
Photo by Steve Mann

Recycling Paper

The U.S. happens to be the largest consumer of paper in the world. And where does all that paper end up? While some does get recycled and reused, the rest makes up a staggering 40 percent of our total waste.

Although 90 percent of the printing and writing paper we use comes from virgin tree fiber, you do have options with recycled paper, which comes in many forms. Recycled paper has labels indicating its percentage of recycled content. But you should know that the universal recycling symbol (three arrows forming a Möbius loop) is used to indicate different things: that the paper is recyclable, made entirely of recycled content, or made partially out of recycled content. Paper with a recycled label can actually be a mixture of virgin wood fiber, pre-consumer waste (scraps from the paper manufacturing process), or post-consumer waste.

Post-consumer waste (PCW) is waste paper that has served its intended purpose and has been separated from solid waste to be recycled into new paper. This is what you and I take to the recycling center. Recycled paper containing PCW is the best paper to buy, as it uses and creates demand for paper that would normally end up in the landfill.

An even greener alternative to PCW recycled paper is paper that has been certified by the Forest Stewardship Council (FSC). Forests that meet the standards set by the FSC are audited at least annually to ensure compliance with the FSC's goals of environmentally appropriate, socially beneficial, and economically viable forest management. Products bearing the FSC seal are guaranteed to be made from wood from a certified well-managed forest (or recycled pulp from certified forests).

So what exactly happens from the moment you toss paper in your recycling bin until you buy recycled paper for your book projects?

The real recycling of paper into new paper happens at a paper mill. Paper mills sort the various paper grades—such as newspapers and corrugated boxes—shred the sorted paper into bits, mix it with water and chemicals, and heat it until a mushy substance called pulp is formed. The pulp is then cleaned and sometimes de-inked to remove ink and sticky materials. Next, the freshly cleaned pulp is refined. Depending on the type of paper being made, the pulp may also need to be bleached.

While paper recycling isn't yet as efficient as glass and metal recycling, its estimated to be 40 percent more efficient overall than making paper from scratch, causing 74 percent less air pollution and 35 percent less water pollution. Plus, every ton of paper recycled saves more than 3.3 cubic yards of landfill space.

Paper isn't the only product made from recycled paper. Filters, insulation, food service products and containers, tissue products, mailing materials, and office supplies (such as pencils) are all excellent bookmaking supplies that can be made from recycled paper.

Cereal Box Books

Designer: Rhonda Miller

Save mini cereal boxes from the trash; they make a
great home for pages made from old maps, discarded
notebooks, and old calendars. Need a bigger book?
Eat your way through a family-sized box.

Finished dimensions

2³⁄₄ x 4⁵⁄₈ inches (7 x 11.8 cm) each

Materials

3 mini cereal boxes

Templates (pages 138 and 139)

About 50 sheets of assorted
recycled papers

1 piece of scrap paper

Blue, red, and yellow linen thread

1 large cereal box

Tools

Basic Tool Kit (page 8)

Stitch

Long stitch (page 132)

Creating the Cover

1 Dismantle the mini cereal boxes by separating the glued edges, and open
them so that the boxes lie flat.

2 Working on your cutting mat, use a utility knife and ruler to trim the small flaps
off the top and bottom of each box. Trim the sides so that only the box front,
box back, and one side remain. The one remaining side will be the spine.

3 To make a punch template for the spine, enlarge the spine template so it's the
same height and width as the spine.

4 Place the template on the spine of one box. Use the awl to poke holes
through the template and through the box. You'll have four rows, each with
six holes. Repeat for the other two boxes.

TIP: When poking the holes, it is best to start on the outside of the box so that the
divot of cardboard created by the hole will be hidden on the inside of the book.

Making the Text Block

5 The paper for the pages needs to be cut to fit inside the covers. The pages
should be twice the width of the cover and the same height, minus ¼ inch
(6 mm) in each direction. Using your utility knife and ruler, trim all your
assorted papers to the appropriate size. You will need 36 sheets for each
book (or 108 total for all three books).

6 Gather the sheets into six stacks of six sheets each. Fold each stack in half and
crease it with the bone folder. You may want to press the folded sections under
a weight overnight to compress the folds and make the sections lie flatter.

7 To make a punch template for the pages, copy the signature template onto
a piece of scrap paper, and cut the paper so it's the same size as the text
block pages. Reverse the fold so that the marks are on the inside, insert this
template into the middle of a section, and use the awl to poke a hole through
the fold at each mark. Repeat this step with each section.

Assembling the Book

8 Cut a piece of linen thread that is about eight times the height of the book,
and thread the needle.

9 Attach the sections to the cover using the long stitch binding technique.

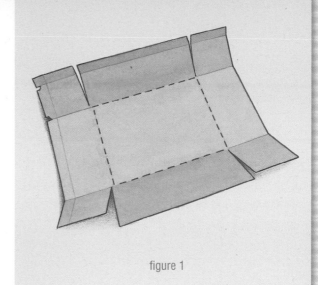

figure 1

Making the Case

10 To make the case, dismantle a large cereal box so that it opens flat.

11 In the center of the box, score four lines to mark off a rectangle that will be the largest side of the case. The rectangle needs to the same height as the book and three times the width of the spine.

12 Mark a strip that measures the same width as each book to each side of the rectangle, and trim away the rest of the box as illustrated (figure 1).

13 Fold and crease each side along the scored lines, and use a utility knife and ruler to cut a narrow notch in each corner.

14 Apply glue to the printed side of the four corner pieces. Fold each side, tuck the pasted corners under the other sides, and burnish the corners with a bone folder. Let the case dry.

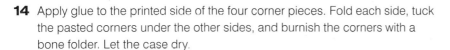

Corrugated Cardboard Journal

Designer: Mauro Toledo

Rugged and sturdy, this book is built for travel, with a wraparound elastic strap to keep it closed on the road.

Creating the Cover

1 Trim your piece of cardboard to 12 x 5½ inches (30.5 x 14 cm). Tear off one side of the cardboard to reveal the corrugation. The top layer will come off easier and in larger pieces in one direction. Test to find the best way to tear it off.

2 Glue the artwork, patterned paper, or photograph to the inside surface of the cardboard. For added thickness, sandwich a piece of heavy cardstock between the cardboard and the paper. Cover the cardboard with wax paper and place under a few heavy books and allow it to dry.

3 Once dry, trim off the excess decorative paper. Measure and mark the following fold lines starting from one short edge and working from left to right: at 4¼ inches (10.8 cm) for the front cover, at 5½ inches (14 cm) for the spine, at 10½ inches (26.7 cm) for the back cover, and at 11½ inches (29.2 cm) for the cover flap. Allow for a little variation, placing the folds between the corrugated waves on the opposite side. Fold along the marked lines.

4 Turn the cardboard over—so the corrugated side is up—and use a piece of removable tape to tape your small cover image in place.

5 Using a craft knife, gently cut through the layer of corrugation around your image without cutting through to the other side of the cardboard.

6 Once cut, peel off the wavy corrugation from the last remaining layer of cardboard.

7 Remove the removable tape from the backside of your cover image. Glue the image in the cover window and allow the cover to dry.

8 Once dry, turn the cardboard face down, with the cover on the left. Measure about 1¼ to 1½ inches (3.2 to 3.8 cm) in from the far right panel edge. With an awl, make a hole or slit (for the elastic) all the way through the lining, cover, and corrugation.

9 Draw a rounded corner on each corner of the flap, and round the corners with your craft knife.

10 Fold the stretch cord or elastic in half, tie the two ends together with a knot, and slip the unknotted side through the hole or slit on the flap. If necessary, reinforce the hole by taping over the knot, and cover the tape with a piece of paper.

Finished dimensions
4¾ x 5¾ inches (12 x 14.6 cm)

Materials
Corrugated cardboard

Printed artwork, patterned paper, or photograph, at least 80 lb. weight and 18 x 7 inches (47.5 x 17.8 cm)

Cardstock

Removable tape

Smaller piece of artwork or photography for window, 3 x 3¼ inches (7.6 x 8.3 cm)

13 inches (33 cm) of stretch cord or elastic

Chipboard, book board, or thick compressed cardboard, 1¼ x 5½ inches (3.2 x 14 cm)

Forty 8½ x 11-inch (21.6 x 27.9 cm) sheets of paper

Graph paper

71 inches (180.3 cm) of hemp or linen binding thread

Tools
Basic Tool Kit (page 8)

Stitch
Long stitch (page 132)

11 Glue the small piece of chipboard, book board, or thick compressed cardboard to the inside of the spine. Allow the cover to dry under heavy books.

Making the Text Block

12 Cut the sheets of paper in half so you end up with pages that are 8½ x 5½ inches (21.6 x 14 cm).

13 Fold each sheet in half. Nest the pages into groups of eight to make 10 signatures.

Assembling the Book

14 Cut a piece of graph paper to the size of the spine reinforcement, and tape it to the chipboard, book board, or compressed cardboard that is already securely glued into the spine.

15 Draw a long stitch design—or go with a basic version—onto the graph paper.

16 Place the towel on your table, and use the awl to push through the marked spots on your spine until you have poked all the holes for each of the 10 signatures.

17 Center each signature vertically in the cover. Using the spine as a guide, mark and punch holes in the signatures so they line up with the holes in the spine and sit centered in the cover when you begin to bind.

18 Complete the book with the long stitch binding technique.

Slightly Frayed Books

Designer: Margaret Couch Cogswell

Fabric is an unusual choice, but a wonderful canvas for an artful
book cover. Recycle that flannel shirt you can't wear in public any
longer or a treasured childhood dress you can't throw away.

Finished dimensions

5 x 4½ inches (12.7 x 11.4 cm)
(smallest); 8½ x 8 inches
(21.6 x 20.3 cm) (largest)

Materials (for one book)
Fabric scraps (old clothing, linens, etc.)

1 to 2 yards (.9 to 1.8 m) of muslin or
other fabric

Sewing thread, 2 or 3 colors

12 sheets of recycled, copier,
or drawing paper

3 sheets of decorative paper or tissue

Scrap paper (larger than your
book cover)

1 yard (.9 m) of 3- or 4-ply thread,
waxed or unwaxed

1 to 2 felt squares in matching
or contrasting colors

Decorative buttons (optional)

Tools
Basic Tool Kit (page 8)

Iron and ironing board

Sewing machine (optional)

Straight pins

Sewing needles

Stitch
Pamphlet stitch (page 132)

Creating the Cover

1 Decide your book size, which might be dictated by the size of the fabric you are using. For your first book, don't go larger than 12 inches (30.5 cm) (closed) in any direction; smaller dimensions make for a more stable book.

2 Pick a background fabric, and tear (if using cotton fabric) or cut it to the size you want. The torn edges create a raw, but finished edge. Pull off any loose threads. For a finished book that is 7 x 7½ inches (17.8 x 19 cm), create an overall cover size of 15 x 7½ inches (38.1 x 19 cm), which includes a 1-inch (2.5 cm) allowance for the spine.

3 Cut or tear shapes for the design on your cover, keeping in mind that the full cover will be folded in half as a finished book. Set the shapes aside.

4 Pick fabric for the inside cover. Cut or tear it to the same size as the outside cover.

5 To add stability to your cover, tear or cut one, two, or three layers of fabric (in this case, muslin) to the same size, or slightly smaller, than the inside and outside covers, to use as layers between the covers.

6 Iron all of the fabric and shapes if necessary.

7 Place the interior layers between the inside and outside covers, and pin them in place. Machine or hand-sew the layers together using horizontal, vertical, or random patterns and making sure to sew within ¾ to 1 inch (1.9 to 2.5 cm) of the outside cover edge so the layers will not flap. You can also sew straight or zigzag stitches along the raw edges if desired.

8 Arrange the shapes on the cover and attach them by hand or machine sewing, or a combination of the two.

Making the Text Block

9 Measure the cover to determine how big to make your pages. The page is the size of the open cover minus 1¼ inches (3.2 cm) horizontally and ½ inch (1.3 cm) vertically. Cut or tear the paper to these page dimensions.

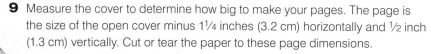

10 Put four sheets together, and fold them in half. Use a bone folder to set the fold. Repeat this step until you have three signatures.

11 Cut or tear decorative paper or tissue to use as end sheets for each signature; these can vary in size.

12 To create a punch template, cut a piece of scrap paper that is the same height as your book and 4 inches (10.2 cm) wide. Fold the paper in half vertically. Mark places for five evenly spaced holes in the center of the fold ½ inch (1.3 cm) in from the top and bottom and no more than 3 inches (7.6 cm) apart.

13 Using the template and an old phone book as a cradle, punch holes in the signatures with an awl, pin tool, or extra-large needle.

Assembling the Book

14 Fold the cover in half and mark the inside center fold line with a straight pin. Open the cover and lay it flat.

15 Place the open middle signature along the fold line of the open cover. Insert the awl into the center hole of the middle signature and through the cover. Leave the awl in place in the hole. Use awls to punch the next two holes; this allows you to punch the holes while the signature and the cover are held in place.

16 Remove the straight pin from the center fold.

17 Cut a piece of linen thread 1 yard (.9 m) long and thread it onto an embroidery needle.

18 Sew the middle signature to the cover using the pamphlet stitch. Cut and tie off the thread with a square knot. Trim the ends to ¼ inch (6 mm).

19 Repeat these steps with the first and third signatures, placing them ¼ inch (6 mm) away from either side of the middle signature.

20 To create a pocket for inside the front cover, cut or tear a rectangle of fabric and fold it in half. Zigzag stitch or finish the edges, and hand-sew the pocket in place.

21 To add a closure, sew a button to the right edge of the front cover. Sew a strip of torn fabric—6 to 8 inches (15.2 to 20.3 cm) long—to the back cover level with the placement of the button.

Scrolling Book

Designer: Reiko Fujii

If you've been following your dentist's advice,
you probably have an empty floss container
lying around; turn it into a clever book with a
single, long wind-up page.

Creating the Cover

1. Open the lid of the dental floss container, and carefully pry up the plastic insert, including the empty floss spool. Remove and discard the metal string cutter and set aside the plastic insert and spool (figure 1).

2. Decorate the container by gluing on paint-stained newspaper, magazine pictures, or recycled paper. Allow it to dry.

Making the Text Block

3. At the bottom of the plastic insert, there is a cylinder (or spokes) that held the spool of floss. Position the plastic insert on the front of the container in the same position as if it was inside the container. Mark the center of the cylinder on the container.

4. Poke a $\frac{1}{16}$-inch (1.6 mm) hole at the mark with the awl. Use the utility knife to scrape off any residual plastic from the hole. The hole should line up with the center of the cylinder when the insert is placed back inside the container.

5. Cut a $\frac{7}{16}$-inch-diameter (1.1 cm) circle—although the size may vary depending on the type of floss box you use—from a $\frac{1}{8}$-inch-thick (.3 cm) piece of eraser to fit tightly inside one end of the empty spool, making sure the spool can still rotate when it is placed back on the cylinder.

6. Cut several $\frac{5}{16}$-inch (8 mm) strips of the used mailing envelope that will fit through the indentation left by the metal string cutter. Carefully attached the strips to each other with tacky glue to make a 10-foot (3 m) strip. Cut a $\frac{3}{8}$-inch (9.5 mm) square of decorated paper, and attach it to the end of the strip that will stick out of the container (figure 2). Let the glue dry completely.

Finished dimensions:
$2\frac{1}{4}$ x $2\frac{1}{2}$ inches (5.7 x 6.4 cm)

Materials
1 empty dental floss container, flat with a short flip top

Tacky glue

Paint-stained newspaper or recycled paper

Eraser

1 large used weatherproof mailing envelope

Cellophane tape

1 small paper clip

Tools
Basic Tool Kit (page 8)

Needle-nose pliers

Wire cutter

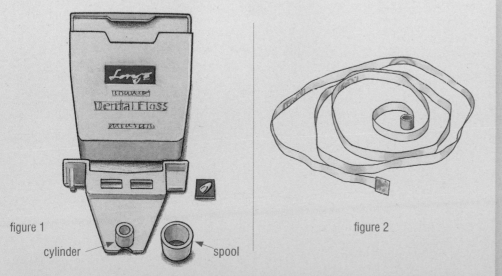

figure 1

cylinder — spool

figure 2

Assembling the Book

7 Securely tape one end of the strip to the spool, and wind the strip around the spool, leaving a 6-inch (15.2 cm) tail.

8 Fit the spool back onto the cylinder. Place the plastic insert and the spool with the attached strip back into the container. Make sure the strip comes out through the indentation on the right side, where the metal cutter used to be. With the decorative square extending out of the left side of the container, pull on the strip, making sure it comes out smoothly.

9 Straighten out the paper clip, and then bend it in half. Bend one end to make a crank handle. Clip the two pronged ends so they are even, and insert the clipped ends through the hole on the front of the container and into the eraser. Slowly wind the strip into the container. Adjust the crank so that the strip winds in smoothly.

10 Pull out the strip and add text and drawings to complete the book.

GALLERY

Mary Ann Sampson
Mona Lisa at the Heart of Dixie Lounge, 1998
Book, 4 x 3¹/₄ x 1¹/₂ inches (10.2 x 8.3 x 3.8 cm)
Cardboard, bubble wrap, bamboo skewers,
toothpicks; piano hinge
Photo by artist

Les Bicknell
Between the Posts, 1998
15³/₄ x 10⁵/₈ x 5¹/₂ inches (40 x 27 x 14 cm)
Found metal, wood from old dairy, paper;
stab binding, paper making, burned
Photo by artist

Game Board Book

Designer: Sara Hindmarch

Long after all the pieces have gone missing, you can still have
fun with your old game boards: use them to create fabulous,
and surprisingly sturdy, Coptic-stitched journals.

Finished dimensions

5¾ x 8¾ inches (14.6 x 22.2 cm)
(largest)

Materials

40 sheets of 8½ x 11-inch
(21.6 x 27.9 cm) recycled/post-
consumer fiber paper

Game board

Metal eyelets in complementary
color (optional)

9 feet (2.7 m) of waxed linen or
hemp thread

Tools

Basic Tool Kit (page 8)

Board punch

Soft vinyl eraser

Eyelet setter (optional)

Stitch

Single-needle Coptic stitch (page 136)

Making the Text Block

1 Fold each sheet of paper in half to 5½ x 8½ inches (14 x 21.6 cm), using the bone folder to smooth the folds flat.

2 Nest the folios together to make 10 signatures of four folios each. Set the signatures aside.

Creating the Cover

3 Measure and cut two sections of your game board to 5¾ x 8¾ inches (14.6 x 22.2 cm). This means the cover will extend ⅛ inch (3 mm) beyond the text block at the top and bottom and ¼ inch (6 mm) beyond the fore edge.

4 Mark a line ½ inch (1.3 cm) in from the spine on the inside of your covers. Then mark 1¼ inch (3.2 cm) in from the head and tail of the covers along this line. Mark four more evenly spaced lines every 1¼ inch (3.2 cm) between those. The result is a line ½ inch (1.3 cm) in from your spine with six dashes 1¼ inches (3.2 cm) apart.

5 Punch a hole at each of the six marks along the spine on each cover. Erase any remaining pencil marks.

6 For a more finished look, set an eyelet in each hole.

Assembling the Book

7 Place one signature of your text block along the inside front cover, aligning the fold with the row of holes and centering it between the head and tail of the cover. Make a mark on the fold of the signature in line with each of the seven holes.

8 Stack your 10 signatures with the marked signature on top, and extend the marks you've made down the spines of all of your signatures. Be careful to keep the signatures squared when marking your lines; if the line down the spines is not straight, the signatures will not line up straight when you sew your binding.

9 Place one signature at a time open on a cutting mat or punching cradle, and use an awl to poke a hole through the spine at each of the six lines.

10 Thread your needle with binding thread. Starting on the inside of your first signature, sew out of the top hole (leaving enough of the tail inside to tie off), through the top hole of your front cover, and back into the top hole of the signature (the same hole you came out of). Tie off your tail inside of the signature, trim the tail, and stitch down to and out of the next hole.

11 Repeat this process of sewing a circle out from your signature, around the cover, back into the signature, and all the way down the spine, stopping when you sew out of the bottom hole. At the bottom hole, sew out of your signature and around your cover as usual, but instead of sewing back into your signature, sew into the bottom hole of your next signature. Sew up to and out of the next hole.

12 Continue assembling the book using the single-needle Coptic stitch with the chain stitch. When you reach the bottom of each signature, remember not to sew back into the bottom hole after your chain stitch, but rather into the bottom hole of your new signature.

13 Once all of your signatures are sewn together with the front cover on one side, place your back cover on top. Sew into the top hole of the cover and back around into your last signature as if you were adding another signature.

14 Sew down to and out the next hole of your signature from the inside, and repeat the process of sewing circles from the signature to the cover. Your thread will end inside the signature on the bottom hole; tie off and cut the tail.

License Plate Book

Designer: Donna J. Engstrom

Use a pair of found license plates—or ones from your
favorite old car—to create the ultimate green
book without a single stitch.

Creating the Cover

1 Wash, dry, and lightly sand the license plates.

Making the Text Block

2 Cut apart the grocery bags and lay them flat.

3 Measure and cut several pieces from the grocery bags that are about ½ inch (1.3 cm) smaller than the length and width of the license plate. Cut plain brown pages and pages from the designs on the bags. Keep scraps to use later as decorative border and trim.

4 If you're using watercolor paper or an old painting, cut them so they're the same size as your grocery bag pages.

5 Lay a license plate on the cut sheets, and use the existing holes as a template to mark the holes—at the top of the pages—for the rings.

6 Punch holes in all the pages using a ¼-inch (6 mm) circle punch.

Assembling the Book

7 Stack the pages in your desired order, mixing painted pages with grocery bag pages.

8 Decorate the pages using grocery sack scraps, the star paper punch, and glitter pens.

9 Assemble the book using the metal rings to hold the front cover, the pages, and the back cover together.

Finished dimensions
12 x 6 inches (30.5 x 15.2 cm)

Materials
5 to 10 brown grocery bags with designs

8 x 12-inch (20.3 x 30.5 cm) scraps of watercolor paper or old paintings

Two metal license plates

Two 1-inch (2.5 cm) binder rings

Matte medium

Tools
Basic Tool Kit (page 8)

Medium-grit sandpaper

Paint palette

¼-inch (6 mm) circle and star paper punches

Glitter pens

Jim Croft and Sustainable Bookmaking in the Old Ways

I like the word *artisan* rather than *artist* to describe what I do since it has involved mostly trying to emulate what others have figured out before me—to make a style of books that embellishes a style developed 500 to 700 years ago during the European Gothic era. I work in this traditional style with a few refinements of my own, and continually strive to make a thick, heavy book that can travel well, open well, and be used for many generations.

I started bookbinding in 1970, and by 1972 I was living rurally without electricity or running water with the goal of making an entire book from raw materials. I immersed myself in the study of hand-powered self-sufficiency in food, fuel, and materials. I admire how simply people have lived throughout history, and I believe we can live that simply again.

Most of my materials are grown or salvaged locally. Trading time for money is ironically appropriate, as the materials I use must often be made instead of bought. A lot of my paper is made from the linen in discarded fire hoses, and I concentrate on hemp and flax fiber because these materials were primarily used during the European Gothic era. Each hose contains many pounds of high quality fiber that can be used to make paper. We also grow our own flax, which makes food, fiber, linen, and linseed oil, and can be used to make beautiful thread.

Straight-grained, quartered, air-dried wood that was used routinely for covers in the old days is nearly unobtainable for money today, but I make my own from raw materials found in firewood and burn piles. I also salvage a lot of high quality paperboard, such as food boxes, file folders, and mailing tubes, for bookbinding. The salvaged material is much more dense and clean than the binder's board, and

it won't dull tools the way purchased board will. Instead of throwing away adhesives when I'm done with a job, I keep sheets of paperboard ready to paste together and press for the next project.

Traditional hand technologies often involve a lot of repetitive use of the body. Since 1972, some of my best times involve the repetitive rhythm of bodywork, such as sawing firewood by hand. Substituting muscle power for electricity or gas motors gives one a freedom that is hard to explain. It goes beyond ancestor empathy—a link is restored between a local world, one's body, and handmade tools making local materials. So far, my wife and I have raised three kids and have had the luxury of choosing the elements of the old ways that we want to use.

As I study the old ways, I am continually amazed that previous generations of craftspeople produced sophisticated goods with primitive tools and techniques, using accumulated wisdom and working with what was nearby. It's my job and passion to rediscover these skills.

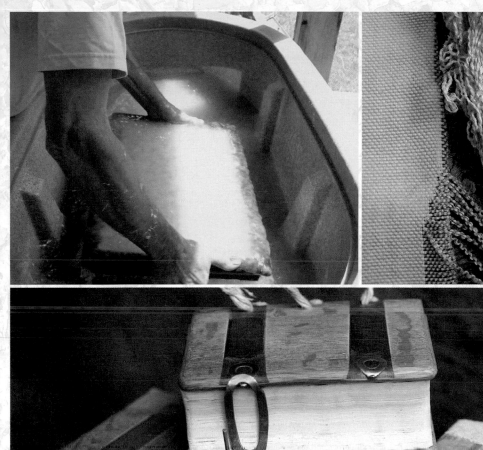

TOP LEFT: Jim Croft immersed in the process of papermaking.
Photo by Shalako Lee

ABOVE: A sampling of Jim's books, made of handmade paper,
brass, wood, and a bit of carving. Photo by Ralph Bartholdt

TOP RIGHT: Fibers reclaimed from the Inside of an old fire hose.

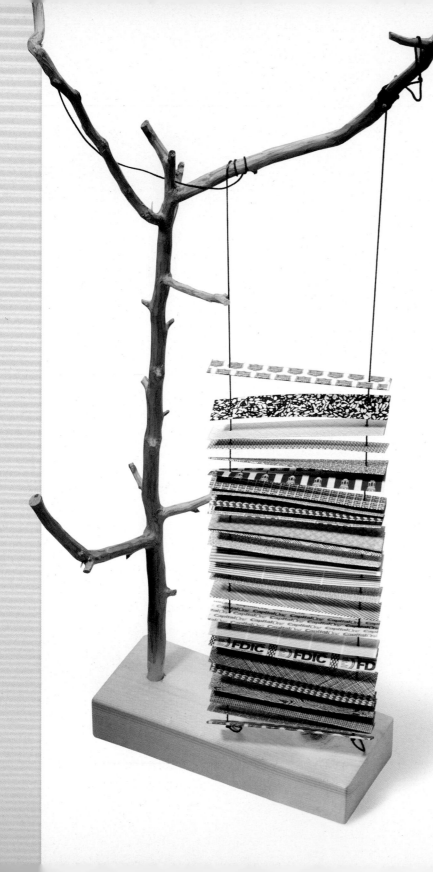

Branching Book

Designer: Mary Ann Sampson

This book/sculpture is based on an Oriental book form—the Palm Leaf Prayer Book—in which sacred texts are scratched into fresh leaves and then smoked over a fire to make the text visible.

Creating the Stand

1 Cut away the leaves and unwanted stems from the oak branch.

2 Remove the bark, and allow the branch to dry for several days.

3 Sand the wooden block base. Drill a hole in the block that's about the same size as the diameter of the tree branch.

4 Put carpenter's glue in the hole, and insert the tree branch. Allow the glue to dry.

Making the Text Block

5 Create the book page insert template by cutting a piece of cardstock to $3/4$ x $4^1/2$ inches (1.9 x 11.4 cm). Poke two holes, each $1/2$ inch (1.3 cm) in from each side edge and 3/8 inches (9.5 mm) from the top and bottom edges.

6 Create the security envelope wrapper template by cutting a piece of cardstock to 2 x $4^1/2$ inches (5.1 x 11.4 cm). Draw a horizontal guide line $1/2$ inch (1.3 cm) from the top, long edge of the template.

7 Cut between 20 and 25 book page inserts, using the template from step 5 as a guide. Do not poke the holes yet.

8 Create the same number of security envelope wrappers by placing the template from step 6 on the non-patterned side of the envelope and cutting out the shape. Mark the guide line across the top of each wrapper.

9 Apply glue to the non-patterned side of the wrapper. Place a book page insert on top, aligning the top of the insert with the guide line.

10 Fold the sides of the wrapper—starting with the top $1/2$-inch (1.3 cm) side first—over the page insert.

11 Repeat steps nine and 10 with the rest of the inserts and wrappers. Put the covered pages between the boards and blotters and weight them. Let the pages dry overnight.

12 When dry, use the book page template to poke holes in the pages.

Finished dimensions
24 inches (61 cm) tall

Materials
Small oak branch, 24 inches (61 cm) tall

2 x 4-inch (5 x 10.2 cm) wood block, about 4 to 6 inches (10.2 to 15.2 cm) in length

Lightweight cardstock (cereal or cracker box)

Security envelopes

Black crochet thread, #5 or #10

Tools
Basic Tool Kit (page 8)

Small garden shears

Hand sander and 100-grit sandpaper

Drill and bit

Carpenter's glue

Pressing boards

Weights

Blotters

Ruler or yardstick

Straight, large-eyed needle

Stitch
Palm leaf binding

eco books

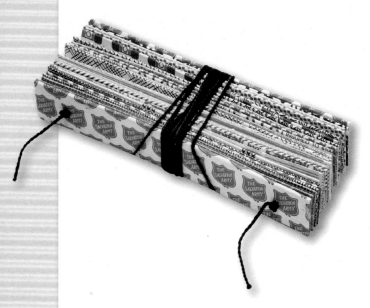

Assembling the Book

13 Measure the space between the tree branch from which you will hang the book and the top of the wood block. Double this measurement, and use it to cut two strands of crochet thread.

14 Working with one thread at a time, tie a triple knot in one end, and thread the opposite end onto the large needle. Sew through one hole at a time, working from the bottom to the top. Repeat this step for the other thread.

15 After both threads are sewn through the book pages, make a loop for hanging and a triple knot in each end of the thread.

16 Hang the book on the selected branch.

Libby Barrett
Pulped Fiction, 2008
Open, 8 x 16 x 5 inches (20.3 x 40.6 x 12.7 cm)
Closed, 8 x 5 x 1½ inches (20.3 x 12.7 x 3.8 cm)
Found paperback book, paper, illustration board; pulped, shaped, letters mounted, accordion fold, glued, impressed
Photo by artist

Margaret Suchland
Ode to Dewey II, 2008
3 x 17 x 5 inches (7.6 x 43.2 x 12.7 cm)
Discarded card catalog cards from various libraries; accordion fold, collage
Photo by Jay Suchland

GALLERY

Tea Time

Designer: Bob Meadows

Do you have a favorite kind of tea to go with your afternoon crumpets?
Use the empty tea box to create a journal that's good any time of day.

Finished dimensions

5 x 3 inches (7.6 x 12.7 cm)

Materials

1 empty tea box, 2¹⁄₆ x 5 x 3 inches
(5.3 x 12.7 x 7.6 cm)

4 sheets of paper, 8½ x 2¾ inches
(21.6 x 7 cm)

Thread, approximately 6 times
the height of the book

Approximately 24 inches (61 cm)
of ribbon

Tools

Basic Tool Kit (page 8)

Stitch

Pamphlet stitch (page 131)

Creating the Cover

1 Open the top and bottom of the box. The front panel, left side, and back of the box will be the front, spine, and back of the book. You can choose which is which.

2 Cut along the right side and flatten the box. With the craft knife, cut away the top, bottom, flaps, and the side not being used.

3 Measure the width of the spine, and divide it into four equal sections. Mark the sections.

4 With the bone folder, heavily score the spine at each of the markings. Then, fold the box into an accordion, creating three valleys and two mountains (figure 1). The signatures will be sewn onto the mountains.

5 On the back cover, decide where you want the ribbon tie. Cut two slits wide enough for ribbon, ¼ inch (6 mm) in from each side and centered top to bottom.

Making the Text Block

6 Fold the pages in half to 4¼ x 2¾ inches (10.8 x 7 cm). Make two signatures with two sheets each.

TIP: If your box is a different size than the one used for this project, calculate your page width by measuring the distance from a mountain fold on the spine to the outer edge, minus ¼ inch (6 mm). The page height should be the height of cover minus ¼ inch (6 mm).

figure 1

Assembling the Book

7 To create a punch template, fold a 1 x ¾-inch (2.5 x 1.9 cm) scrap of paper in half lengthwise. On the fold, measure and mark ½ inch (1.3 cm), 1⅜ inches (3.45 cm), and 2¼ inches (5.7 cm) from the top.

8 Place the template inside the first signature, put the signature in position on the first mountain of the accordion, and reverse the accordion fold. Center the signature so there is ⅛ inch (3 mm) above and below it. Use a cradle or an old phone book, the punch template, and the awl to punch three holes through the signature and spine. Set the signature aside and return the accordion fold to a mountain. Repeat for the second signature on the second mountain fold.

9 Punch holes in the first and last valley folds, centering the template top to bottom as in step 8.

10 Thread your needle. You can use the thread in one continuous piece or cut it into three pieces that are about twice the height of the book.

11 Place the first signature in position on the first mountain fold. Using the pamphlet stitch, attach the signature (figure 2). Repeat for the second signature.

12 To join the covers, sew a pamphlet stitch through the first and last valley folds, beginning at the inside back of the book.

13 Insert the ribbon through the slits on the back cover, starting on the outside, going across the inside, and then back out. Pull the ribbon around the box, even the ends, and tie it in a bow.

figure 2

Mousepad Journal

Designer: Alexia Petrakos

Personalize a plain
mousepad with your own
stencil, and gather some
junk mail, envelopes, old
printouts, and grocery bags
to make journal pages.

Creating the Cover

1 Create a design for your cover, keeping in mind that it will be cut in half later in step 5. Transfer the design to paper, and tape your pattern onto the dull side of a piece of freezer paper. Cut out the design, making sure to go through both the paper pattern and the freezer paper. The freezer paper cut out will be your stencil.

2 Set your iron to dry, medium-high heat, and place the stencil shiny side down on top of the mousepad. Iron the stencil onto the mousepad; press hard but avoid keeping the iron in one place too long.

3 Once the stencil is secure, dab the black fabric paint lightly onto the mousepad. Go over it a couple times if your first application is too light or if you missed spots. Remove the stencil, and let the black paint dry.

4 Lightly outline the design with a small paintbrush and white paint, adding a few highlights.

5 When the white paint is dry, cut the mousepad in half with the craft knife so you have two halves that are $4\frac{1}{4}$ x $7\frac{3}{4}$ inches (10.8 x 19.7 cm).

6 Copy the template, and mark the holes for the mousepad covers. Make sure the *top* of the template is at the head of the book. Use the leather punch to cut the holes.

Making the Text Block

7 Gather your papers—unfolding paper bags and taking apart envelopes you plan to use—and cut 24 sheets that measure 8 x $7\frac{1}{8}$ inches (20.3 x 18.1 cm).

8 Fold each piece in half to create folios, and burnish the fold with the bone folder for a sharp crease.

9 Working one piece at a time, place one folio under the cover with the folded edge lined up with the left edge of the cover. Trace the curve of the mousepad on to the top and bottom right corners of the folded sheet. Cut the corners of each signature to match the mousepad corners.

10 Make six signatures of four sheets each, and mark a small dot on the top corner of each signature. This will mark the head of each signature.

11 Fold the template in half. Using the template and an awl, punch holes in each signature.

Finished dimensions
$4\frac{1}{4}$ x $7\frac{3}{4}$ inches (10.8 x 19.7 cm)

Materials
Freezer paper

Floppy blue mousepad, $7\frac{3}{4}$ x $8\frac{1}{2}$ inches (19.7 x 21.6 cm)

Fabric paint, black and white

Template (page 138)

Junk mail, envelopes, old printouts, or paper grocery bags

Unwaxed black linen thread

Beeswax or white microcrystalline wax

Tools
Basic Tool Kit (page 8)

Iron

Leather punch

Stitch
Multi-needle Coptic stitch (page 134)

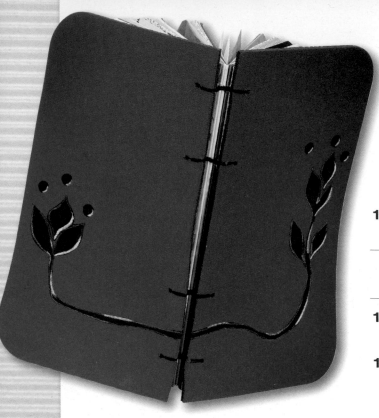

Assembling the Book

12 Cut two lengths of unwaxed linen thread, each four times the height of the book. Run the threads through beeswax or microcrystalline wax three times.

TIP: Microcrystalline wax is a good option for this step because it won't leave a yellow residue, and it doesn't come from bees, which is a plus.

13 Thread and lock the fours needles by inserting the needle into the short end of the thread and pulling it down over the eye.

14 Lay the back cover of your book face down in front of you with the spine closest to you. Open a signature, and working from inside out, thread each set of needles through a pair of holes.

15 Close the signature and place it on top of the back cover of your book, with the folded side facing you. Take the needles into the back cover twice, and loop them around the spine. Pull gently. Repeat for each set of holes.

16 Stack another signature on top of the first signature making sure the marks you made are aligned. Continue assembling the signatures using the multi-needle Coptic stitch.

TIP: Sand down the points of your bookbinding needles so they don't poke holes where they're not wanted (like in your fingers).

17 When you draw the thread out of the last signature, instead of locking the stitch, loop each thread once through the holes in the front cover (figure 1). Tug each one gently to tighten, then pass the thread through two signatures and lock your thread as usual.

18 Draw the threads back up and loop them through the holes in the top cover again. Tie off inside, and trim the ends, leaving about 1/4 inch (6 mm).

19 Dab glue on the knots to secure them, and leave the book open to dry.

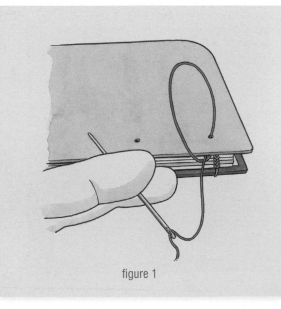

figure 1

Fresh Squeezed

Designer: Julie Gray

An empty orange juice container—or any juice, for that matter—recycles into a cute little box to hold a book all about oranges.

Finished dimensions

3¾ x 2¾ inches (9.5 x 7 cm) closed

Materials

Heavyweight weatherproof paper

Wallpaper paste

Orange acrylic paint

Heavyweight paper

Artificial silk leaf

Various papers in white and orange

Template (page 140)

Orange and white ink or paint

Ultrafine orange ink pen (for lettering or drawing)

Orange seeds and stem

Photos of oranges

High gloss lacquer (optional)

24 inches (61 cm) of orange bookbinding thread

Orange tissue paper

Gallon orange juice carton

Tools

Basic Tool Kit (page 8)

Light box

Colored pencils

Double-sided tape

Stitch

Japanese stab binding (page 132)

Creating the Cover

1 The book cover can be made to match the carton you are using. To make a paste paper cover, mix leftover wallpaper paste with orange acrylic paint, and use it to paint the weatherproof paper.

2 Cut the cover to 2⅝ x 7¼ inches (6.7 x 18.4 cm), and fold it in half.

3 Emboss an *O* on the cover by cutting a 2-inch-tall (5 cm) *O* shape out of heavyweight paper. Lay it on a light box and center your paper cover over it. Press gently around the shape with the point of a bone folder or a burnisher.

4 Glue on the silk leaf so the letter looks like an orange, and use the colored pencils to add dimension and shading.

Making the Text Block

5 Cut the orange and white papers to 2½ x 3½ inches (6.4 x 8.9 cm). Decorate them with a combination of photos, quotations, calligraphy, orange seeds, ephemera relating to oranges, and various recycled materials. Make sure to leave at least ¼ inch (6 mm) at the top of your pages free of design for stitching.

6 When your pages are decorated, slip them inside the folded cover.

7 With the awl, punch three equally spaced holes ¼ inch (6 mm) down from the top.

Assembling the Book

8 Bind the book with the Japanese stab binding technique using orange bookbinding thread.

9 Wash and dry your empty orange juice container.

10 Slice off the bottom panel with the utility knife, and then slice up the side where the seam is, pulling apart the top carefully.

11 Keep the lid screwed on, and on top, score and cut the carton following the template (figure 1). Crease the scored folds with your bone folder.

12 Wad up a piece of orange tissue paper and then flatten it out. Stick the paper on the inside bottom of the box with double-sided tape. Place your book inside the tissue paper.

13 Cross over the two side flaps, fitting them together at the slices. They should fit to the exact width of the box (figure 2).

14 Fold down the top with the lid on, and then fold over the bottom flap. The hole cutout should fit right over the lid to hold the box snugly closed.

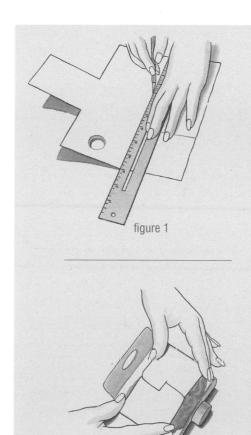

figure 1

figure 2

Office Supplies Book

Designer: Sara Hindmarch

Held together with rubber band binding,
this book makes the most of used office
supplies: the messier, the better.

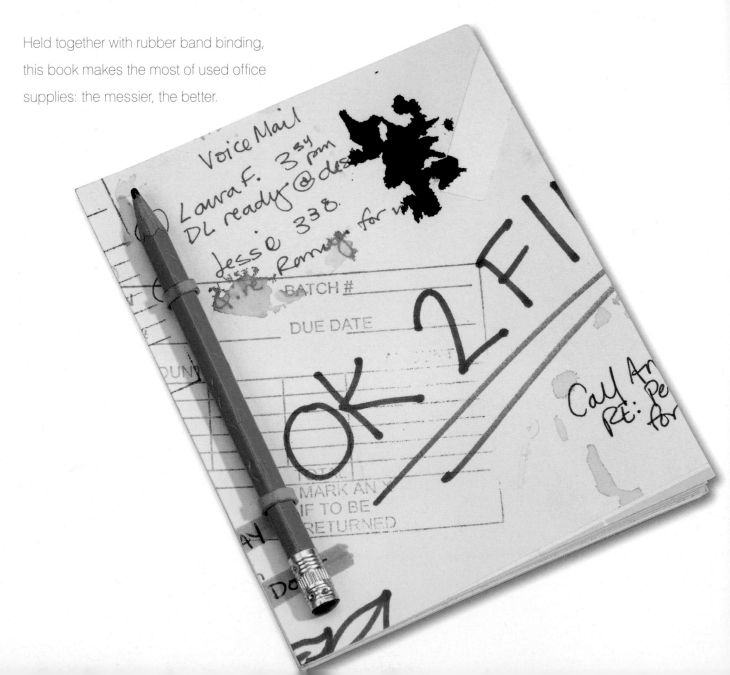

Creating the Cover

1 Keep an old file folder destined for the trash on your desk, and mark up the surface with notes, misprinted file labels, coffee spills, invoice stamps, and other accumulated markings until one side is fully layered with decoration.

2 Cut the decorated side of your folder into two 4¼ x 5½-inch (10.8 x 14 cm) pieces.

3 Decide which piece will be the front and which will be the back. On the long left edge of the front cover, mark two spots: one 1 inch (2.5 cm) below center and one 1 inch (2.5 cm) above center, both ½ inch (1.3 cm) in from the spine edge. Set the cover aside.

Making the Text Block

4 Fold each sheet of paper in half lengthwise, with the printed side facing in. Each folded sheet will measure 4¼ x 11 inch (10.8 x 27.9 cm).

5 Cut the folded sheets in half widthwise, so that you end up with two folded 4¼ x 5½ inch (10.8 x 14 cm) halves. You should create 30 folded pages total.

Assembling the Book

6 Stack the 30 folded sheets together, with the folded edges aligned and facing toward the right. Place the front cover on the top and the back cover on the bottom of the stack, with the decorated sides facing out and the marks on your front cover at the left edge.

7 Tap the edges of the stack on the table a few times to make sure everything is aligned and squared. Clamp the stack together with a binder clip along the right folded front edge.

Finished dimensions
4½ x 5½ inches (11.4 x 14 cm)

Materials
Manila file folder, standard letter size

Assorted file labels, invoice stamps, markers, and other office supplies

Pencil stub, 4 to 5 inches (10.2 to 12.7 cm) long

15 sheets of 8½ x 11 inch (21.6 x 27.9 cm) single-side printed *junk* paper

Rubber band, ¼ inch (6 mm) wide

Tools
Basic Tool Kit (page 8)

Hole punch

8 Punch a hole through your stack at the two marks on the spine edge. Be sure you are punching holes along the non-folded long edge.

> **TIP:** If your hole punch can't cut through the whole stack at once, use the front cover as a template to punch holes a few sheets at a time, using the binder clip to hold the pages together.

9 Thread the rubber band through the holes so that the loops poke up through the two holes on the front cover and the length of the band runs along the back cover.

10 Insert the pencil through the loops on the front cover, and remove the binder clip. The tension of the rubber band and pencil will hold the book together.

Julie Mader-Meersman
Date Night, 2008
4¼ x 8½ x ⅝ inches
(10.8 x 21.6 x 1.6 cm)
Discarded coupon pages, laser print, recycled paper grocery bag, surplus conveyor belt rubber; discarded paperboard packaging fragments; flagbook, accordion spine
Photo by artist

Patchwork Portfolio

Designer: Sara Hindmarch

Take a cue from the quilting world and turn your paper scraps
into a colorful cover for a Coptic-stitched journal.

Finished dimensions

5 7/8 inches (14.9 cm) square

Materials

40 sheets of assorted paper, old book pages, and junk mail, 11 x 5½ inches (27.9 x 14 cm) or larger

1 sheet scrap mat board, 11½ x 5¾ inches (29.2 x 14.6 cm) or 2 pieces at least 5¾ inches (14.6 cm) square

4 sheets lightweight mulberry paper, two 6¾-inch (17.1 cm) squares and two 5¼-inch (13.3 cm) squares

Assorted decorative paper scraps

Wax paper

Scrap paper

Eyelets (optional)

4 lengths of 2½-foot-long (.8 m) waxed linen or hemp thread

Tools

Basic Tool Kit (page 8)

Board punch

Eyelet setter (optional)

Stitch

Multi-needle Coptic stitch (page 134)

Making the Text Block

1 Cut each piece of assorted paper to 11 x 5½ inches (27.9 x 14 cm). Fold the pages in half, and arrange them into 10 signatures of four folios each. Set the signatures aside.

Creating the Cover

2 Measure and cut two sections of your mat board to 5¾ x 5¾ inches (14.6 x 14.6 cm). The covers will extend ⅛ inch (3 mm) beyond the text block at the top and bottom, and ¼ inch (6 mm) beyond the fore edge. Set the boards aside.

3 On each of your larger square sheets of lightweight mulberry paper, create a patchwork pattern with your assorted decorative papers; ½ inch (1.3 cm) of the design will wrap around each edge of your cover.

4 Carefully glue all of your pieces in place on the mulberry paper, keeping a sheet of wax paper underneath to prevent it from sticking to your table. Peel your finished covers off slowly, and press them overnight between fresh sheets of wax paper.

5 To form your endpapers, repeat steps three and four with your 5¼-inch-square (13.3 cm) mulberry sheets.

6 Place the dried covers, paper face down, on a piece of scrap paper and apply a thin layer of glue, starting at the center and brushing outward. Center your first cover board down on the glued sheet so that there is paper overhanging on each edge. Gently lift the cover and smooth flat any bubbles or puckers with your bone folder.

7 Place the cover face down on your scrap paper, and fold in each corner to create a little square on the inside of the cover. Dab a little glue on the top corners and fold the sides in. Use your bone folder to smooth down the edges (figure 1).

8 Apply a thin layer of glue to the back of one endpaper, and center it on the inside of the cover you've just made.

9 Repeat steps five through seven to create the second cover.

10 Wrap each completed cover in wax paper and press them under heavy books; let them dry overnight.

Assembling the Book

11 On each cover, mark two dots ½ inch (1.3 cm) in from the spine at ¾ inches (1.9 cm) in from the head and tail. Mark an additional dot ½ inch (1.3 cm) in from the spine and 1 inch (2.5 cm) in from each of these marks. Punch a hole through each of the four dots on the front and back covers. Set an eyelet in each hole to give your book a more polished look.

12 Place one signature of your text block along the spine of the inside back cover. Center the signature so there's ⅛ inch (9.5 mm) extra above and below. Mark the spine of the signature in line with each of the four holes.

13 With the marked signature on top, stack your 10 signatures and copy the marks you've made down the spines on all of your signatures. Be careful to keep the signatures squared when marking your lines.

14 Open one signature at a time, and place it on a cutting mat or punching cradle; poke a hole with your awl through the spine at each of the four lines.

15 Tie two of your binding threads together at their ends, then repeat with the other two threads, so that you have two long threads. Make sure that the resulting two threads are the same length, trimming off any excess tails from where the threads are tied together.

16 Thread each of your four needles so that you have one needle at each end of each piece of thread. Starting from inside the first signature, sew out of each hole. Make sure your threads are all the same length once you have come out of the signature, and your knot is centered between the two holes (figure 2).

17 Sew through the holes in your front cover, from the outside to the inside. Wrap your threads once around themselves to hold the stitch and carefully tighten your threads. Wrap your thread around to the same side—left or right—each time to keep your stitches uniform.

18 Place your next signature on top, and sew into the holes aligned with each of your threads. Continue attaching signatures using the multi-needle Coptic stitch.

19 To add the back cover, sew through the holes from the outside to the inside and wrap your threads to hold the stitch. Lift the last signature with your back cover, wrap your thread around the stitch aligned with each thread, and then sew back up into each hole of the last signature that your thread exited.

20 Tie each thread to its end mate inside the signature and trim off the tails.

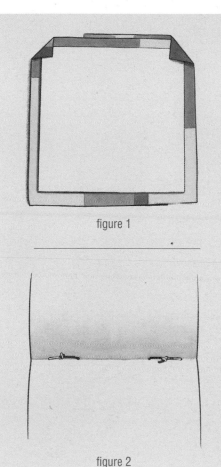

figure 1

figure 2

Produce Tray Book

Designer: Erin Zamrzla

Next time you purchase a packet
of portobellos, don't toss the
tray; instead, use it to make a
fabulous recycled book.

Creating the Cover

1 Lay the produce tray face down on a cutting mat. Find the center of the tray, and use the ruler and pencil to draw a line parallel to the short sides.

2 Using the metal ruler and a sharp utility knife, carefully cut along the line, dividing the tray into two equal parts. These pieces will serve as the front and back covers for your book.

3 Make pencil marks for four holes on each tray. Measure ½ inch (1.3 cm) in from the cut edge and 1 inch (2.5 cm) from the top and bottom of the flat portion of the tray (the point where the tray no longer curves), and make two marks for holes. Space two more holes equally between the top and bottom holes.

4 Punch the holes in both covers with the hole punch (figure 1).

5 Set an eyelet into each hole, making sure that they face out. The eyelets will prevent the cardboard from tearing when you sew the pages to the covers.

Making the Text Block

6 Because each produce tray varies in size, you must customize the size of the pages to fit the tray. To begin, cut your paper scraps to about the same size as the tray (before you cut it in half).

7 Fold each page in half, smoothing each fold with the bone folder.

8 Nest together 10 pages along the folded edges to create one section. Repeat with the rest of your pages.

9 Place the covers together as they will be when the book is completed. Measure the distance between the covers. This is how thick your text block should be.

10 Stack together several sections until the stack's height is equal to the measurement from step nine. Don't push down on the pages; just hold them loosely in place. This is the number of sections that will be in your book. Save an extra section or two in case the measured stack compresses while being sewn.

11 Measure the height and width of the cover, and subtract ½ inch (1.3 cm) from the height and ¼ inch (6 mm) from the width. Use the ruler and utility knife to trim the center section—and any extras—down to this measurement.

12 The sections on either side of the center section will become gradually smaller. Trim each successive section ⅛ inch (3 mm) smaller than the previous section on the top, bottom, and fore edge. Check the stack as you trim the sections down, making sure that they fit within the cover.

Finished dimensions
4 x 5 inches (10.2 x 12.7 cm)

Materials
Cardboard produce tray*

8 matching ⅛-inch (3 mm) round eyelets

120 or more text-weight or slightly heavier paper scraps, about the same size as the produce tray

80 inches (203.2 cm) of 4-ply waxed linen thread in any color

*Do not use any container that housed meat.

Tools
Basic Tool Kit (page 8)

⅛-inch (3 mm) hole punch

⅛-inch (3 mm) eyelet setter

Stitch
Multi-needle Coptic stitch (page 134)

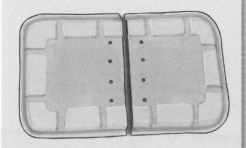

figure 1

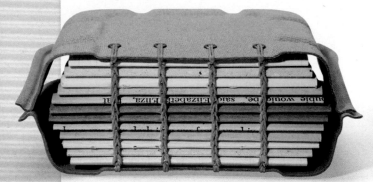

13 Once all sections are cut to size, create a punch template using the cover holes as a guide. Lay one of your extra folios against the inside of one of the covers, centering it between the top and bottom. Make four pencil marks along the folded edge of the folio exactly in line with the four holes in the cover.

14 Use the template—making sure it's centered—to punch holes in all the signatures, starting with the smallest signature first. If you wish to round the corners of your signatures, now is a good time to do so; use a corner rounder or a pair of scissors.

Assembling the Book

15 Begin to bind the book using the multi-needle Coptic stitch.

16 When you have sewn half of your pages into the cover, check to see if the thickness of the text block is equal to the depth of the front cover. If they are equal, continue to sew. If they are not equal, adjust the number of signatures appropriately. If your text block is thinner than the cover, you may need to add a section or two to the center. If your text block is thicker than the cover, you may need to remove the center section.

17 Continue binding the book.

Lemon Tree Linen

Designer: Annie Fain Liden

This dos-a-dos book makes a fabulous showcase for vintage treasures—from buttons to embroidered fabric—and green finds alike, including a crafty use for walnuts.

Finished dimensions

6 x 11½ inches (15.2 x 29.2 cm)

Materials

3 old book covers or 6 large cereal boxes

2 secondhand, embroidered fabric pieces

1 yard (.9 m) of vintage botanical print fabric

Black and tan sewing thread

Recycled, chlorine-free text paper

Reused brown packaging paper

Walnut dye

Black and mint green Irish waxed linen thread

Two salvaged decorative buttons

Tools

Basic Tool Kit (page 8)

Ripping knife

4 curved binding needles

Stitch

Multi-needle Coptic stitch (page 134)

Creating the Cover

1 Create three 6 x 11½-inch (15.2 x 29.2 cm) hard covers by gluing layers of cereal boxes or covers cut from old books—the uglier, the better—together until you reach a thickness to your liking. Put some weight on the glued layers so they dry flat.

2 Cut the embroidered fabrics and four pieces of vintage fabrics into 9 x 13½-inch (22.9 x 34.3 cm) pieces. Use a needle and black sewing thread to add hand-embroidered details and embellishments to further enhance the design of the secondhand fabrics.

3 Place one embroidered fabric on top of one piece of vintage fabric with the right sides together, and hand or machine sew both sides and the top with a 1¹/₁₆-inch (2.7 cm) seam allowance. Repeat this process joining the other embroidered piece with one vintage fabric piece and joining the remaining two pieces of vintage fabric.

4 Slide one cover into one of the fabric pockets to make sure it's a good fit. If it is, trim the seam allowances and the corners to reduce excess bulk. Turn all three of the fabric pockets right side out. Slide each cover into a fabric pocket. Tuck the seam allowances inside and whipstitch the pockets closed.

Making the Text Block

5 Make a template that is the size of a single page. The height should be ⅛ inch (3 mm) shorter that the length of the covers and two times the width minus ¼ inch (6 mm).

6 Use the template, a bone folder, and a ripping knife to rip 60 text pages from large sheets of recycled text paper. To create a signature, fold a pile of six pages in half. Make 10 signatures total.

7 Rip six pages from a scrap piece of brown packaging paper, using the template, bone folder, and ripping knife. Wrap a brown paper page, or insert, around the outside of six of the 10 signatures. Set the folds with your bone folder and put the entire pile of signatures under a heavy book or weights.

8 Make a shallow batch of diluted walnut dye, and dip the fore edge of each signature in it, giving each page a warm brown tip.

9 Make a template that measures 1 x 11½ inches (2.5 x 29.2 cm) for marking holes in the covers and signatures. Along a long edge of the template, make a mark ¾ inch (1.9 cm) from the top and bottom. Then make a mark 2½ inches (6.4 cm) in from each of the first two marks. There will be four marks total.

10 Place the template, with the marks to the left side, ¼ inch (6 mm) in from the left edge of the cover. Use an awl to punch the holes. Do the same with the right side of the back cover, and both the left and right sides of the center cover.

11 After all the cover holes are punched, trim ⅛ inch (3 mm) off the bottom of the template. Using an old phone book as a cradle, place the template inside one signature, lining up the bottom edges, and punch four holes through the center fold. Repeat with all 10 signatures.

Assembling the Book

12 Divide the signatures into two piles with five signatures (three with brown paper inserts) in each pile, alternating the plain and brown-paper-wrapped signatures within each pile. The embroidered fabric covers are the front and back book covers; the vintage fabric cover goes between the two piles of signatures and inserts.

13 Measure two lengths of mint green and two of black waxed linen thread, each measuring half the height of the book times the number of signatures plus one full length of the book.

14 Start stitching the front cover and its first signature with the multi-needle Coptic stitch, working your way to the center cover. Repeat for the back half of the book.

15 To create a button closure, place one button on the right edge of the cover. Punch two holes with an awl, and sew the button in place. Then use an awl to punch a hole straight across from the button in the center cover.

16 Tie the ends of a scrap of black and mint waxed linen together; put the black thread through the hole in the center cover, and tie a knot. Create a variegated twine by twisting both threads to the right and passing the right thread over the left as illustrated (figure 1). Wrap the variegated twine around the button to close the book. Repeat for the back cover.

"GREEN" DYE

Making your own walnut dye is easy. Simply steep collected nut husks in hot water until you get the color you want, cool and strain the water, and you're ready to go. Save unused dye in glass jars.

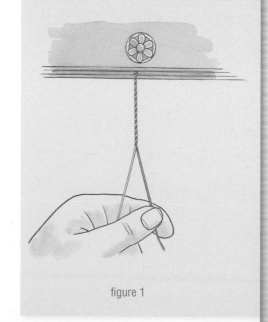

figure 1

Redux Books

Designer: Michelle Francis

Ever thought about taking apart an old book to make a new one?
That's just what this project does, using recycled paper pages
and lotka wraps.

Creating the Cover

1 Open the book to the table of contents; cut away the front and back covers with the utility knife, taking care to separate and preserve the end sheets. These can be used as new pastedowns for the inside covers of the journal. If they are unsuitable for pastedowns, consider saving any bookplates for reuse in the journal. Discard the text block for recycling.

2 With the micro spatula, carefully lift up and remove the outside edges of the original pastedown on the inside of the front cover. Next, carefully remove the remnants of the material covering the original spine. Lightly sand the inside cover and spine area—but not the decorative book cloth—to smooth out uneven areas and to remove residual glue. Glue down any corners or edges of the book cloth that have come loose. Repeat with the back cover (figure 1).

3 Cut two 2 x 9 inch (5.1 x 22.9 cm) strips of lokta paper to use as spine wraps for the covers. On each cover, lightly mark and then score a line where you want the long edge of the spine wrap to be glued. The scored line should be the same distance from the fore edge of the front and back covers.

4 Glue the spine wrap to the front cover using the scored line as a guide and centering the strip head to tail. Smooth out the strip with a bone folder. Turn the cover over and trim the remaining edges to ⅝ inch (1.6 cm). Miter the corners, and glue the edges of the strip to the inside cover. Use your fingernail or a bone folder to tuck the paper around the corners. Repeat with the back cover.

5 Cut paper for new pastedowns from the salvaged end sheets or from the remaining lokta paper. Each pastedown should be ¼ inch (6 mm) smaller than the height and width of the cover. Glue pastedowns to the inside covers, smoothing out wrinkles with a bone folder. Place wax paper on the glued side of the covers, and put weight on them until they're completely dry, preferably overnight.

Making the Text Block

6 Cut the office paper so it measures the height of the book cover minus ¼ inch (6 mm) and twice the width of the book cover minus ¼ inch (6 mm). Fold five sheets at a time into nine separate signatures. Set the folds with a bone folder, and lightly number the signatures in the upper right-hand corners.

7 Cut nine strips of lokta paper so each is 1½ inches (3.8 cm) wide and the same height as the signatures. These will be wraps for each signature.

Finished dimensions
5 x 7¾ inches (12.7 x 19.7 cm)

Materials
Old hardback book

1 or 2 sheets of lokta paper, about 30 x 19 inches (76.2 x 48.3 cm)

Wax paper

45 sheets of 24- to 30-pound office paper, 8½ x 11 inches (21.6 x 27.9 cm) (at least 30 percent post-consumer recycled)

Cardstock

Template (page 140)

Scrap book board or plywood

2 or 3 rubber bands

Tools
Basic Tool Kit (page 8)

Scalpel

Micro spatula

Fine grit sandpaper

Hand drill with ¹⁄₁₆-inch (1.6 mm) drill bit

Curved sewing needle

Stitch
Single-needle Coptic stitch (page 136) with kettle stitch (page 134)

eco books

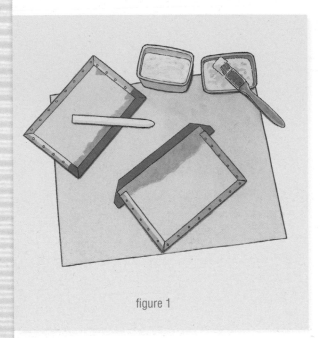

figure 1

8 Fold the signature wraps in half lengthwise, and place one around each signature. Copy the template onto scrap cardstock. Use the cardstock template and the awl to punch holes in the signatures.

Assembling the Book

9 To punch the holes in the covers, lay the cardstock template on the front cover with the left-hand edges lined up and centered. With an awl, mark the holes by punching through the template. Remove the template. The marks should be ½ inch (1.3 cm) in from the spine edge. Use rubber bands to hold the covers together with right sides out. Working over the scrap book board or wood, hand drill holes through both covers using a ¹⁄₁₆-inch (1.6 mm) drill bit.

10 Remove the rubber bands, and stack the signatures in order between the covers.

11 Cut a length of thread that is the height of the book times the number of signatures, plus five more heights of the book.

TIP: Always pull, or snug, your thread in the direction you are sewing to avoid ripping through the holes.

12 Begin stitching the book by placing the back cover face down in front of you, with the last signature (signature 9) on top and the spine edges facing you. Open the signature to the center and pull your needle and thread through the bottom hole (hole seven), which will be on your right-hand side. Leave a 3-inch (7.6 cm) thread tail.

13 Bring your needle up through the bottom hole in the cover and out between the inside of the cover and the signature, but to the right of the thread coming out of the signature. Snug up the thread. Go back in through the bottom hole of the signature. Tie a square knot with the tail. Trim the tail, leaving at least ½ inch (1.3 cm). Go out hole six (the one to the left). Repeat the previous step, ending with the thread coming out between the signature and the back cover at hole one. Don't go back into hole one.

14 Place the next signature (signature 8) on top of signature nine. Open the signature to the center, and pass the needle through hole one and out hole two.

15 Pull the thread through. Hook your needle around the thread connecting the back cover and signature nine. Open up the back cover to be certain you have sewn around, and not between, both connecting threads, and that you have not snagged those threads with your needle. Close the book, snug the thread, and insert the needle back into hole two of signature eight. Exit hole three and repeat, ending with the thread coming out of hole seven of signature eight.

TIP: Always hook away from the direction you are sewing—as if you were going back to the last hole instead of going forward to the next.

---

16 The stitch at the head and tail of the signature is a kettle stitch. Hook the needle back around the thread connecting signature nine and the back cover. Instead of going back into hole seven of signature eight to create a chain, bring your needle through the loop you have created and snug up the end of the two signatures.

17 Repeat steps 13 through 16 and continue adding signatures, ending with your thread coming out of hole seven of signature two. Complete the kettle stitch, but do not add signature one.

18 Signature one and the front cover are sewn together, so position them both on top of your text block. Insert the needle down through hole seven of the front cover; it will come out between the inside of the cover and signature one on the right side of the thread. The thread should be loose, not snug. Cross over the thread, and go into hole seven of signature one and out hole six. Carefully tighten the thread beginning with the one that is coming out between the cover and the signature.

19 Hook the thread back as if to make a chain as in previous rows, but instead of going back into hole six, take your needle up through the loop as if you were doing a kettle stitch. Snug the thread, and then bring your needle down through the cover, as in the previous step, on the right side of the thread. Don't snug the thread. Cross the thread over and into hole six of signature one and out hole five. Repeat the ending with the thread on the inside of hole one of signature one.

20 Make certain the thread is snug. To tie off the thread, make two half-hitch knots on the inside around the thread between holes one and two. Trim the tail, and erase all the pencil marks on the signatures.

Junk Mail Journal

Designer: Leslie Hart

Junk mail goes from trash to treasure
once freshly inserted—no stitching
required—between the pages of an
old hardback book.

Creating the Cover

1 Remove the pages from the inside of the hardback book with a craft knife.

2 Lay the book cover flat on its back so you can cover the inside entirely with paper (or fabric). Cut the paper or fabric to the exact size of the flattened book minus a little from each edge so that the material doesn't run over the edge of the book. Protect your work surface with wax paper, and glue the paper to the book.

3 To create a new spine, cut a piece of stiff cardboard the same height and thickness as the pages you removed. Measure and cut a piece of paper or fabric 1 inch (2.5 cm) longer and wider than the cardboard. Place the cardboard in the middle of the paper or fabric, and wrap it around the edges of the cardboard; glue the edges down (figure 1).

4 Decide how many signatures you want in the book, and use a nail and hammer to make that number of holes in the covered cardboard spine.

5 String the waxed bookbinding thread through the holes, ending with both ends on top of the spine

6 Apply glue to the back of the spine, and lay it on the book with the thread ends up (figure 2).

Making the Text Block

7 Cut pages from the junk mail and other found papers into the appropriate size for the book. Fold the paper into signatures, and arrange them into three stacks.

Assembling the Book

8 Place each signature over the thread on the spine, and tie the thread off in the middle of each signature. Repeat until finished.

Finished dimensions
5 x 8½ inches (12.7 x 21.6 cm)

Materials
1 used hardback book

Scrap paper or fabric

1 piece of stiff cardboard

Found papers or junk mail

Wax paper

Bookbinding thread

Tools
Basic Tool Kit (page 8)

Paper cutter (optional)

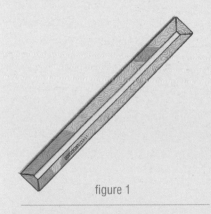

figure 1

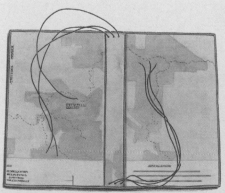

figure 2

Elemental Book

Designer: Bob Meadows

Combining a bit of earth and fire—in the form of
rocks and matchsticks—this stab bound book
creates a humble homage to the natural world.

Creating the Cover

1 From the scrap mat board, cut two $7\frac{1}{4}$ x $5\frac{3}{4}$-inch (18.4 x 14.6 cm) pieces; two 1 x $5\frac{3}{4}$-inch (2.5 x 14.6 cm) pieces; and two $8\frac{5}{8}$ x $5\frac{3}{4}$-inch (21.9 x 14.6 cm) pieces. Glue each of the pairs with right sides together, and place them under weights to dry.

2 Cut the two bags from top to bottom, on the seam, and cut away the bottom. Wad up the bags tightly, wet them thoroughly, and then squeeze hard to remove the excess water. Open up one bag and smooth it out. Tear off a piece of wax paper and place it under the wet bag.

3 Brush watercolors randomly on the wet bag using plenty of pigment. Set the bag aside to dry on the wax paper. Repeat with the second wet bag.

TIP: When using lighter color paints, let the paper dry on newspaper instead of wax paper.

---

4 To decorate the front cover, create your own design with matchsticks or copy the one in the sample, using figure 1 as a guide. Lay the $7\frac{1}{4}$ x $5\frac{3}{4}$-inch (18.4 x 14.6 cm) board horizontally in front of you, and glue the matchsticks in place; you may need to trim the bottom sticks (figure 1). Let the glue dry thoroughly.

5 When the bags are dry, iron them with a medium-heat iron, but don't get rid of all the wrinkles. Cut two $10\frac{1}{4}$ x $7\frac{1}{4}$-inch (26 x 18.4 cm) pieces from the darker bag to serve as the cover papers. Cut two $8\frac{1}{2}$ x $5\frac{1}{2}$-inch (21.6 x 14 cm) pieces from the other bag to serve as the liners for the inside covers.

6 Lay one of the cover papers—with the side you want to show face down—on the table. Draw a horizontal line $\frac{3}{4}$ inch (1.9 cm) up from bottom and $\frac{3}{4}$ inch (1.9 cm) from the left side. This is where you will place the cover.

7 Apply glue to the front cover board (over the matchsticks). Place the cover, with the matchstick side down, along the $\frac{3}{4}$-inch (1.9 cm) marks and press firmly. Turn the cover over, and press the paper over the sticks with your fingers and a bone folder.

8 Turn the cover paper back over. Apply glue to the 1 x $5\frac{3}{4}$ inch (2.5 x 14.6 cm) board and position it on the paper to the right of the pasted board. Make it even with the bottom of the first piece, leaving a $\frac{3}{8}$-inch (9.5 mm) gap for the hinge. Miter the corners, fold them back over the board, and crease.

Finished dimensions
$8\frac{5}{8}$ x $5\frac{3}{4}$ inches (21.9 x 14.6 cm)

Materials
Mat board scraps

2 brown paper lunch bags or other brown paper, 5 x $10\frac{5}{8}$ inches (12.7 x 27 cm)

Wax paper

Watercolors

22 used wooden matchsticks (with the tip trimmed off) or twigs

Text paper, any number of pages cut to $8\frac{1}{2}$ x $5\frac{1}{2}$ inches (21.6 x 14 cm)

Thin pliable wire

5 small pebbles

1 larger flat stone, about 1 to $1\frac{1}{2}$ inches (2.5 to 3.8 cm) in diameter

Tools
Basic Tool Kit (page 8)

Iron

Drill or large nail and hammer

Needle-nose pliers

Stitch
Japanese stab binding (page 132)

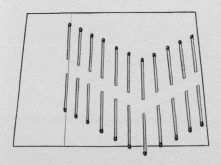

figure 1

Our Home!...
the Earth

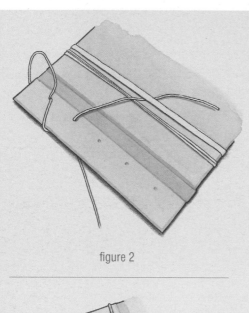

figure 2

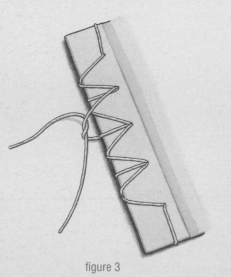

figure 3

9 Continue working your way around the cover, gluing over the edges and corners and burnishing.

10 Apply glue to the back of one of the 8½ x 5½-inch (21.6 x 14 cm) liner papers. Place the liner paper on the cover board so it is ⅛ inch (3 mm) shorter than the cover on 3 sides—but flush on the spine edge—and burnish. If the paper stretches and is too long, trim the spine side to fit. Repeat steps 4 through 10 to make the back cover.

Making the Text Block

11 Score all the text block pages 1⅝ inches (4.1 cm) from the spine edge for easier reading.

12 Cut two 8½ x 5½-inch (21.6 x 14 cm) pieces from the wax paper used to dry the bags to create the text cover sheets. Place one on the front of the text block and the other at the back.

13 Line up the text block pages as perfectly as possible. Wrap a 2 x 13-inch (5 x 33 cm) piece of scrap paper around the text block—top to bottom—and tape. This will hold the pages in position while you drill and sew them.

Assembling the Book

14 Place the text block on the back cover, flush to the spine edge, leaving about ⅛ inch (3 mm) around the other sides. Carefully place the front cover atop the text block, lining it up with the back cover. Secure the layers with rubber bands or clips.

15 Prepare a punch template on a 5¾ x 1-inch (14.6 x 2.5 cm) piece of paper. Measure ¾ inch (1.9 cm) from the left edge, and draw a line. Then, on the line, measure down ⅞ inch (2.2 cm), 1⅞ inches (4.7 cm), 2⅞ inches (7.7 cm), 3⅞ inches, (9.8 cm) and 4⅞ inches (12.4 cm). Punch points with an awl to mark drilling the points, and then drill holes large enough for your thread to pass through three times, through the book layers.

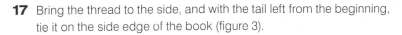

16 Thread the needle and begin to sew from the front through the second hole from the top, leaving a 5-inch (12.7 cm) tail. Go around the spine and in the top hole from the front; then go around the head of the book and back into the first hole (figure 2). Continue assembling the book using the Japanese stab binding technique.

17 Bring the thread to the side, and with the tail left from the beginning, tie it on the side edge of the book (figure 3).

18 Cut five lengths of wire—such as 24 gauge brass wire—that are about 3 to 4 inches (7.6 x 10.2 cm) long. Wrap each of the small pebbles well enough so it won't fall out, and make a loop in the end using needle-nose pliers.

19 Separate the tail strings into several threads (or add more strings if yours will not separate), and attach a wrapped pebble to each. Attach a larger stone on the front of the book using contact cement.

Margaret Suchland
Artifacts II, 2008
3¼ x 18 x 4 inches (8.3 x 45.7 x 10.2 cm)
Discarded historical glass positive photographic plates from a natural history museum; accordion fold tunnel book
Photo by Jay Suchland

Bar Notes

Designer: Mauro Toledo

On your next trip to a bar or restaurant, harvest a few supplies for this cool book project, assembled with a matching set of coasters and a decorative long stitch.

Creating the Cover

1 Trim a 1-inch-wide (2.5 cm) strip from one of the three coasters, preferably in the middle away from the rounded corners, to make the spine.

2 Cut three strips of colored tape to approximately 9 inches (22.9 cm) long, and place them side-by-side on your work surface, overlapping the edges and with the sticky side up. Position the spine on the tape between the two coasters. Wrap the tape around the spine and the edges of the two coasters, bending the extra tape at the top and bottom edges.

Making the Text Block

3 Trim three 6½ x 3½-inch (16.5 x 8.9 cm) pieces of paper from each sheet of paper. You should end up with 66 pieces of trimmed paper for your pages.

4 Fold all the interior pages in half to create 3½-inch-square (8.9 cm) pieces of paper.

5 Stack eight pieces of the folded paper inside one another to create eight signatures. You can discard the two extra sheets.

Assembling the Book

6 Trim the piece of graph paper to the size of the spine—approximately 1 x 3½ inches (2.5 x 8.9 cm). Using removable tape, attach the paper to the outside of the spine.

7 Use a pencil to draw your long stitch design on the graph paper. Use dots to mark where you want the holes for the binding to be (figure 1).

8 Fold a towel in half and then in half again to protect your table top, and place the covers face down on the towel.

9 Push the awl through the dots you created in step seven, making sure you are going lightly through so that the holes are not too stretched out.

10 Center each signature vertically in the cover. Use a pencil to mark where you want the hole in the signature to be so that it lines up with the holes in the spine and sits centered in the cover when you begin to bind. Repeat this step with the remaining signatures.

11 Bind the book using a long stitch binding technique.

Finished dimensions
3¾ x 3½ inches (9.5 x 8.9 cm)

Materials
3 beer coasters, approximately 3½ inches (8.9 cm) square

¾-inch-wide (1.9 cm) tape, to match the coasters

22 sheets of 8½ x 11-inch (21.6 x 27.9 cm) paper

Graph paper

Towel

Colored linen or hemp thread, in a contrasting color

Tools
Basic Tool Kit (page 8)

Stitch
Long stitch (page 132)

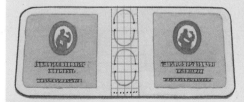

figure 1

Shopper's Joy Book

Designer: Rhonda Miller

The world may not need another plastic bag, but here's a clever and eco-friendly idea for reusing them: iron several layers of shopping bags together to create book covers.

Making the Text Block

1 Cut open and flatten the paper bags.

2 Working on a cutting mat, use a ruler and a utility knife to cut the paper bags into 36 rectangles that are 7 x 4¾ inches (17.8 x 12 cm).

3 Arrange the sheets into six piles, with six sheets in each pile. Fold each pile to create the six signatures for the book. Crease the folds with a bone folder, and press the six sections under a weight.

4 Copy the signature template onto scrap paper. Insert the template into the middle of a signature, and poke a hole through the fold at each mark with an awl. Remove the template and repeat to make holes in the remaining signatures.

Creating the Cover

5 Preheat the iron to a low setting—such as for nylon or silk. Use scissors to trim off the bottom edge and handles of the plastic bag. Cut one side edge to create a large rectangle.

TIP: If there is any printing on the bag, turn it inside out; having colors on the outside will make a mess during the ironing. Words and images printed on the bag usually still show through from the back.

---

6 Spread the bag on the table, flattening and smoothing it with your hands. Fold the bag in half, and in half again. Continue folding it into smaller rectangles until the bag is about 10½ x 5¼ inches (26.7 x 13.3 cm) and between eight and 10 layers thick.

7 Sandwich your plastic rectangle between two sheets of newspaper. Start ironing on top of the newspaper (never put the iron directly on the plastic!), slowly back and forth, and over and over. After a couple of minutes, the moving layers should start to bond together. If it looks like nothing has happened, your iron temperature is too low, however if the iron is too hot, the plastic will contort dramatically on contact. Continue ironing until the layers of plastic have bonded together into a consolidated plastic sheet, which can take five to 10 minutes depending on how many layers of plastic you have. You might need to flip the plastic over if the bottom layers aren't bonding.

8 When the plastic is completely bonded, it should be the correct size and shape for your book cover. Let it cool for a few minutes. If it's too big, trim it with scissors or a utility knife.

Finished dimensions
3½ x 5¼ inches (8.9 x 13.3 cm)

Materials
8 to 10 brown paper bags

1 plastic shopping bag

2 sheets of newspaper

Templates (pages 138 and 139)

Red all-purpose thread

1 piece of scrap paper

Linen bookbinding thread

2 gray buttons

Tools
Basic Tool Kit (page 8)

Iron

Sewing machine

Stitch
Long stitch (page 132)

eco books

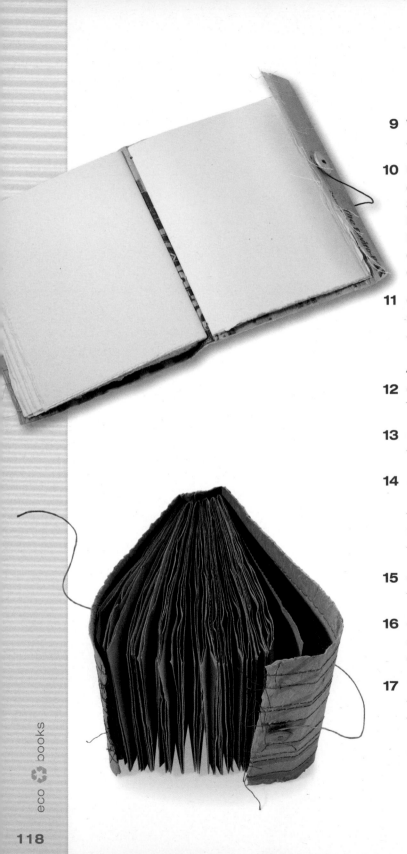

9 With a sewing machine and red thread, add rows of decorative stitching back and forth across the cover.

10 Using a bone folder and ruler, score four fold lines on your plastic cover to create the various sections of the wraparound cover. The first line should be 3¾ inches (9.5 cm) in from the left edge (to create the front cover); the second line should be ¾ inch (1.9 cm) from the first line (to create the spine); the third line should be 3¾ inches (9.5 cm) from the second line (to create the back cover); and the fourth line should be ½ inch (1.3 cm) from the third line (to create the wrap-around flap). Fold and crease the cover at each score line.

11 Copy the spine template onto scrap paper. Center the template onto the spine area of the cover, and use the awl to poke a hole through the template and through the cover at every point where the template lines intersect.

Assembling the Book

12 Cut a piece of linen thread that is about eight times the height of the book. Thread the needle.

13 Place the cover on the table in front of you so that the back cover is on the table and the spine is toward you.

14 Place one signature inside the book so it's aligned with the first row of holes (closest to the back of the book). Starting from the outside of the book, insert the needle through the first hole (at the top of the book) of the first row of holes. Pull the thread through the cover and the corresponding hole in the first signature, leaving a tail about 5 inches (12.7 cm) long.

15 Go back through the second hole of the signature and the cover, and pull the thread through until it's snug.

16 Continue working with long stitch until you exit the last hole of the final signature. Secure the ends of the threads by tying them together. Trim the ends, or leave them long to embellish later.

17 Using 18 inches (46 cm) of linen thread, sew one button to the center of the front cover and the other button to the wraparound flap, tying the threads on the back. With the last stitch, take the thread back through the cover material (but not back through the button) so that the thread comes out between the button and the cover material to create the tie.

Plein Air Sketchbook

Designer: Geraldine Pomeroy

With sturdy cardboard covers—complete with a handle—and a handy spot for colored pencils, this sketchbook is ready to follow you anywhere your artistic muse takes you.

Finished dimensions

13³/₁₆ x 8¹/₁₆ inches (33.5 x 20.5 cm)

Materials

Used paper bags (brown or white)

Packing box cardboard

Petroleum jelly

Woven cotton twill tape

10 gold split pin fasteners

Natural string, 1 length per signature height plus 12 inches (30.5 cm)

3 colored pencils

Tools

Basic Tool Kit (page 8)

Rubbing cloth

Stitch

Coptic stitch (page 134)
with a kettle stitch (page 134)

Making the Text Block

1 Line up and trim the bags to 9¹/₂ x 8 inches (24 x 20 cm), leaving the base fold of the bag intact.

2 Fold the pages in half, and insert four folios inside one another to assemble your signatures.

3 Stack your signatures and mark six sewing points on the spine in pencil. Make one mark 1 inch (2.5 cm) in from both ends and two more pairs of marks in the center of the spine, slightly wider than the twill tape. Also mark the tape positions on the back cover.

4 Open up each signature and gently punch through all the pages on the marked points.

Creating the Cover

5 Trim your cardboard to 13³/₁₆ x 8¹/₁₆ inches (33.5 x 20.5 cm) so the packaging box handle grips are on the right edge. This allows for a ³/₈-inch (9.5 mm) overhang on the top, bottom, and left edge.

6 Seal the cardboard by gently massaging petroleum jelly on both sides, letting the petroleum jelly soak in for 15 minutes and then gently rubbing off the excess with a cloth.

7 Cut two pieces of twill tape to your required length—enough to come over 3 inches (7.6 cm) on the back, around the spine width, and long enough onto the front cover to accommodate the pencils. Secure one strip of twill tape to the back cover with a split pin and glue. Repeat for the other tape. Be sure to glue right up to the cardboard edge, and then let dry.

Assembling the Book

8 Once the tapes are dry, turn the back cover face down so the tapes are underneath. Place the first signature on top and align the holes with the tape.

9 Thread your needle with the string and tie a knot on one end.

10 Enter through the far right hole from the outside, and sew into the signature. Proceed to the next hole and bring the needle out over the tape and back into the next hole. Repeat at the next hole and sew out, over the tape and back into the signature. Proceed to the final hole and exit the signature. Pull the thread taught.

11 Place another signature on top and enter through the first hole immediately above your last exit point. Repeat until you reach the last hole and exit. Before adding another signature, loop around and back under the stitch—forming a kettle stitch—to secure the two signatures together. Proceed until all the signatures are sewn onto the tapes. The last exit stitch is a double kettle stitch. Tie a knot and snip off the excess thread. Pull the tapes taught to ensure that all the stitching is nice and firm.

12 To attach the tape to the front cover, pierce a hole through the tape and cover. Place the split pin through the hole, and glue along the edges and back of the tape all the way to the edge of the cover. Repeat with the other length of tape.

13 Slide a pencil in place next to the split pin, place the tape over it, and mark off the next split pin point. Pierce the tape and cover, push the pin into the tape, glue behind the pin top on the tape, and push the pin through the cover. Repeat this process for the rest of the spit pins and the other length of tape.

14 Once they're glued in place, trim off the tapes to your desired length and glue the ends down well. Let dry. Slide your pencils in place.

The Coffee Book

Designer: Gail Stiffe

Created using a simple carved linoleum stamp and
the palm leaf binding technique, this round book fits
perfectly in its coffee tin container.

Making the Text Block

1 Trace the perimeter of the coffee tin onto the cardstock. Draw a line ³⁄₁₆ inch (5 mm) in from the outer edge of the circle, and cut this line to create a template for your pages.

2 Cut about 60 discs from different kinds of paper using the template.

TIP: Soak the white paper in coffee for an hour to soften the color.

---

3 Cut the linoleum slightly smaller than your page template, and draw a design—in this case, a coffee cup—on top, remembering to reverse your image. Cut out the design with the cutting tools. Use the printing ink or acrylic paint and the brayer to print your image onto some of the pages.

4 Use the awl to punch two holes, 1½ inches (3.8 cm) apart, along the diameter of the template. Use the template to punch holes through all of the pages, and arrange them in your preferred order.

Creating the Cover

5 Cut two discs of mount board the same size as the pages. Cover the outside of the mount boards with decorative paper and the inside with plain paper. Cut the decorative paper slightly larger than the mount board and the inside paper slightly smaller. Center and glue the mount board on the wrong side of the decorative paper and snip into the paper at regular intervals. Fold the paper over the edge of the mount board. Glue the plain paper to the other side of the mount board to cover the edges of the decorative paper. Repeat with the second mount board. Use the template and the awl to make holes in the covers that align with the holes in the text block.

Assembling the Book

6 Thread the fishing line in through the front cover, through all of the pages and the back cover, then back through the other hole in the back cover through to the front cover. Make sure you leave about 11¾-inch (30 cm) of ease so that the pages of the book can expand.

7 Even up the lengths of the fishing line. Thread both through the large bead, and then thread one end through the small bead. Tie the ends around the small bead by wrapping the end of the fishing line around the other line and back through the formed loop. Do the same with the other end of the line, trapping the bead between the knots.

8 To cover the tin with a printed piece of paper, measure the height and circumference of the tin, and cut a rectangle of paper to that size, adding ¾ inch (2 cm) to the circumference. Use glue or double-sided tape to attach the paper to the tin.

Finished dimensions
3½ inches (8.9 cm) in diameter

Materials
Coffee tin

Light cardstock (for template)

Paper, including a mix of brown craft paper, handmade paper, and coffee filters

Coffee

Linoleum

Printing ink or acrylic paint

Mount board

Fishing line

2 beads: one large, one small

Recycled cartridge paper

Tools
Basic Tool Kit (page 8)

Linoleum cutting tools

Drayer

Baren

Stitch
Palm leaf binding

Exposed Stitch Scrap Book

Designer: Gail Stiffe

This exposed stitch book turns remnants and scraps into
the main attraction: a fine home for your poetic musings.

Making the Text Block

1 Prepare at least six signatures of between three and five sheets folded in half.

2 Make a punch template for the signatures and the cover by cutting a rectangle of cardstock 1³/₁₆ inches (3 cm) wide by the length of the signatures. Fold the template in half lengthwise, and mark sewing stations in the fold. Mark the top station about ⁵/₈ inch (1.6 cm) from the head and the bottom station ³/₄ inch (2 cm) from the tail. Mark other stations between these two that are at least 1³/₁₆ inches (3 cm) apart, so that you end up with an even number of stations. The stations can be evenly spaced or form a pattern. Use the template and the awl to punch holes in all the signatures.

Creating the Cover

3 Cut two pieces of cardboard ¼ inch (6 mm) taller and ⅛ inch (3 mm) wider than the folded signature pages.

4 Cover the cardboard with fabric using either glue or double-sided tape. Wrap the fabric around three sides of the cardboard, but leave the spine edge so the fabric and cardboard are flush.

5 Line each of the covers with the recycled paper.

6 Cover the back of a piece of soft leather with strong double-sided tape (leaving the backing on), and cut a strip from the leather that's about 2³/₈ inches (6 cm) wide by twice the height of your book.

7 Stack your signatures (six is a good number), and measure the depth of the stack when it is loosely held. Cut a piece of cardstock that is this measurement wide by the height of your cover.

8 Center the cardstock spine on your piece of leather, and cut lightly around it in order to remove the backing from the taped area under the card. Remove the backing, and press the cardstock spine down onto the tape.

9 Remove the rest of the backing from the tape, and place your covers in position on the leather spine. It is a good idea to do this on a grid to ensure that your covers are lined up and that you have even spaces on either side of the cardstock spine. Fold the top and bottom of the spine to the inside, trimming the leather so that both ends are flush on the inside of the cover.

Finished dimensions
4¹/₂ x 5³/₄ inches (11.4 x 14.6 cm)

Materials
30 sheets of 5¹³/₁₆ × 8⁵/₁₆-inch (14.8 x 22.7 cm) (size A5) recycled paper, folded in half

Cardstock

2 pieces of cardboard

Remnant of upholstery fabric

2 sheets of 4¹/₈ × 5¹³/₁₆-inch (10.5 x 14.8 cm) (size A6) recycled paper (for lining the covers)

Scrap of leather, 13³/₄ x 2³/₈ inches (35 x 6 cm)

Double-sided tape (with peel-off paper backing)

Linen or embroidery thread, 2 colors

Tools
Basic Tool Kit (page 8)

Stitch
Exposed stitch binding

figure 1

Assembling the Book

10 Align the template from step 2 with the leather spine, and cut slits in the leather to correspond with the holes in the signatures. Make sure you leave ⅛ inch (3 cm) at the top and bottom of the signatures to allow for the overlap of the covers.

11 Cut about 1 yard (.9 m) of waxed cotton or linen thread, and thread it through a tapestry needle.

12 Start inside the top hole of the first section, take the thread out through the corresponding slit, over the top of the book, and back into the top hole. Tie off the loose end, then go into the next hole down, out through the slit, and then back into the hole below, continuing to the tail of the book.

13 Now go out through the bottom hole and slit, then into the bottom hole of signature 2, back around over the tail of the book, and out through the second hole from the bottom. Continue in this way until all the signatures are attached, and tie off the thread at the last hole.

14 Using a contrasting thread, start inside the top hole of the first signature, and tie the end to one of the threads already there. Take the thread diagonally across to the second hole of the last signature, back up to the first hole of the last section on the inside, and then diagonally across to the second hole of the first section to make an X.

15 Now take the thread on the inside to the third hole of the first signature, diagonally to the fourth hole of the last signature, inside to the third hole of the last signature, and diagonally to the fourth hole of the first section to make another X (figure 1).

16 Continue in this way to the bottom of the book and tie off.

Second Thoughts:
A Recycled Story

Designer: Nancy Pobanz

Pages from a discarded book and a bicycle inner tube
are given new life together as a hinge-mounted book.

Finished dimensions

2 x 6 inches (5 x 15.2 cm)

Materials

16 pine boards, 2 x 6 x ⅜ inches
(5.1 x 15.2 x 1 cm)

Sandpaper

Old book

Acrylic soft gel matte medium

Buff acrylic paint

Acrylic matte medium

Thin bicycle inner tube

18-gauge wire nails, ⅝ inch
(1.6 cm) long

Cigar box with sliding lid, and inside
dimensions 5 x 6¼ x 3⅜ inches
(12.7 x 15.9 x 8.6 cm)

Paper to line the inside of the cigar box
(optional)

Wax medium (optional)

Tools

Basic Tool Kit (page 8)

Hammer

Small, motorized drilling tool and a
⅛-inch-high (3 mm) engraving tip

Creating the Cover

1 Sand all six sides of each piece of pine.

2 Select and remove 16 pages from an old book. With soft gel acrylic medium, adhere each page, text side up, to a board. When adhering the paper, be careful to align the text with the top and bottom edges of the boards.

3 Using a cutter with a sharp blade, trim the paper flush with the board's edges. Holding a bone folder at a 45° angle, press along all four trimmed edges to be sure the paper edges are in total contact with the wood.

4 Dilute the acrylic paint with acrylic medium, and paint over the text to soften the words. Allow the boards to dry thoroughly overnight or longer.

5 Incise the surface of each text-covered board with the drill, roughly imitating handwriting. Hold the drill vertically (like a pencil) and carve into the wood through the paper. The carved lines should run parallel to the lines of text, but they don't have to be completely straight.

6 Clean the dust from the incised lines using a dry, stiff brush. Burnish the surface, using a bone folder to push down any raised spots.

7 Seal the entire surface of the paper and the carved lines with acrylic matte medium. Burnish the surface with wax paper to prevent sticking later on.

8 Leaving the edges bare, coat the backside of each board with homemade or store-bought paint; this may take several layers. Allow the paint to dry thoroughly and then apply a final coat of acrylic matte medium to seal the pigment.

Assembling the Book

9 Cut the inner tube into two 2 x 10-inch (5 x 25.4 cm) pieces, and clean them with soap and water.

10 To attach the inner tube hinges, set up a solid, square frame to support the piece while nailing; the designer used scraps of flat marble found as discards at a local stone retail business. Place one board at a time in the support with the left edge facing up and working from left to right, with the back cover board first (on the left) and the front cover board last (on the right).

11 Starting with the back cover board, begin attaching the rubber hinge to the pages as illustrated (figure 1). Place the first rubber hinge about ½ inch (1.3 cm) down from the top edge and flush with the cover's surface. Working ⅜ inch (9.5 mm) in from the rubber's edge, gently pound the nail through the rubber and into the wood, working carefully to avoid splitting the wood or ending up with the nail poking out somewhere.

12 Gently pound the second nail through the rubber, into the board directly across the piece of rubber, so the rubber is attached to the board with two nails.

13 Place another board next to the first one and pound two nails through the rubber into that board, as in steps 11 and 12. Continue adding the rest of the boards and attaching them to the first rubber hinge with two nails. Do not stretch the rubber, but make sure it lies flat. Trim any extra rubber flush with the last board.

14 Attach the second rubber hinge in the same manner, close to the bottom edge of the pages.

15 Cut out the book's title, or print your own, and glue it onto the cigar box lid. For a finished look, glue the lining paper into the box, and apply a wax finish to the outside surfaces. Position the book in the box and the box lid on top of the book.

PIGMENT PERFECT

Can't find the perfect hue in the store? Make your own paint using a found rock, a stone mortar and pestle, acrylic medium, and water. First break the rock into chunks—goggles are a good idea—and grind it in the mortar and pestle. Sift the powder with a sieve onto a smooth surface, and mix the pigment with water and acrylic medium.

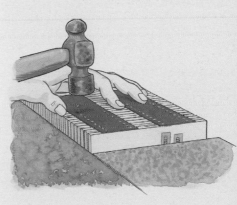

figure 1

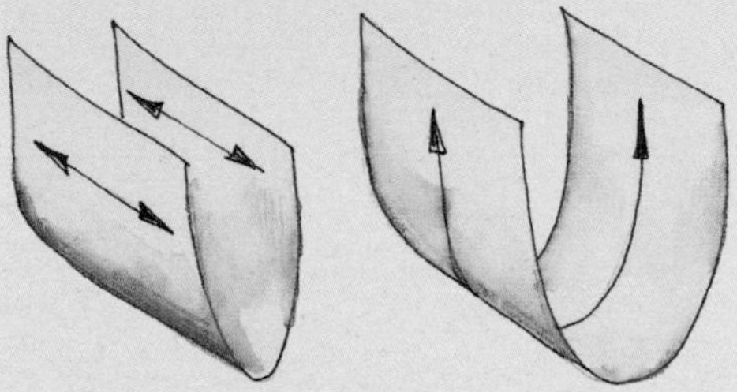

figure 1

figure 2

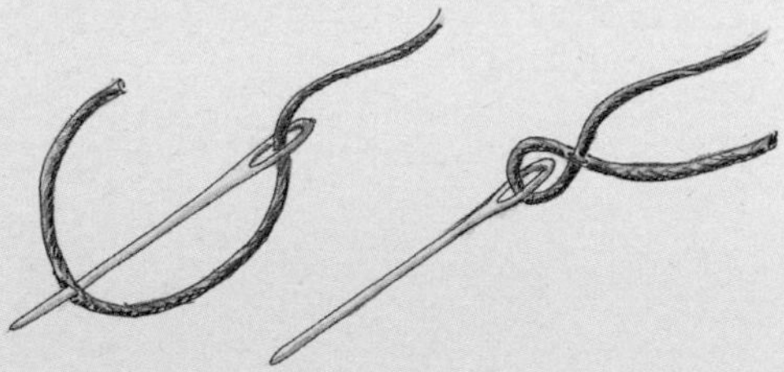

figure 3

appendix

Preparing the Text Block

The folded and sewn pages that make up your book are called the *text block*. For most of the projects in this book, the following directions will serve to prepare the paper for your text block.

Folding and Cutting

You'll want the *grain* of all the papers—indicated with a watermark on some commercial papers—to run parallel to the spine. Folding with the grain is easier and the pages will turn more gently. To determine the grain, fold a sheet of paper into a curved shape, first one way and then the other (figure 1). The grain runs parallel to the smaller curve. If you need to fold against the grain, make sure you fold all the papers for that particular book against the grain.

Sorting

Once your paper is trimmed to size and folded, it's ready to be sorted into signatures. To make a signature, fold each sheet in half, creasing the fold with your bone folder. Gather the sheets together, nesting one inside another. After this step, your paper pages can be punched and stitched.

Punching with a Template

The next step in the bookmaking process is punching the holes—or sewing stations—in your text block and cover. It's not critical that the sewing stations be evenly spaced up and down the spine; in fact, many decorative spines have unevenly spaced holes. However, it is important that the signatures are punched precisely. A template allows you to punch multiple signatures accurately and quickly. A few projects require you to make multiple templates in order to make a decorative stitching pattern on the spine of the book.

To make the template, cut a piece of scrap paper 2 to 3 inches (5 to 7.6 cm) wide and exactly the height of your book. Fold it in half vertically; then measure and punch the holes in the folded edge.

Lay the first signature in an open phone book (a great recycling use for your old phone books), and put the template on top in the fold, aligned carefully with the top of the signature. Punch the sewing stations with an awl. Repeat with the remaining signatures. If you have more than one signature, be sure to maintain their order before you begin to sew them together (figure 2).

Follow the same steps to punch the sewing stations in the cover. Punch the holes, remove the template, and use a clip to hold the pages together to prevent the holes from shifting out of alignment before sewing.

General Stitching Techniques

These directions are very basic and can be used with many different materials. You'll adapt various procedures to achieve the details shown in specific projects. Making green books involves solving the problems created by using unusual materials. After your first few books, you won't need to look at these directions; you'll be able to adapt them for whatever book you envision making.

Paper is more delicate to sew than fabric, and many of the recycled materials you choose to use in your book aren't as strong as traditional book materials. As you sew, you will need to work gently with your materials and possibly make a few adjustments to your standard sewing techniques.

Before you start sewing, coat your thread—if it isn't already waxed—with a bit of beeswax so it slides more readily through the paper. The wax helps to lock the thread onto the needle so you don't mistakenly unthread it while working. After threading the needle, pull a thread tail a couple of inches (cm) from the needle's eye. Pierce this tail with the needle, and slide the thread back to the eye, locking it in place at the eye (figure 3).

Avoid tearing the paper by tightening the thread after each stitch; always pull in the direction the thread is going rather than straight up or backwards.

When you've finished binding the book, don't tie a knot at the end of the thread. Instead, leave a tail a few inches (cm) long and tie it off at the end of the stitching. In a few cases—long stitch and Coptic binding, for example—the tail is tied off after a few signatures are attached. This is because the stitching doesn't come back to the beginning as it does with simple stitches, such as the pamphlet stitch.

Pamphlet Stitch, 3 hole

This simple structure is used for smaller books, usually no taller than 6 inches (15.2 cm) and with a small number of pages. After you've punched holes—approximately 1 inch (2.5 cm) from the head and tail of the book and another one half way between them—in the text block and the cover, clip the pages together to prevent the holes from shifting.

To complete the most basic "*butterfly*" pamphlet stitch, cut a piece of thread that is two times the height of the book plus a few extra inches (cm), and thread a needle. Do not tie a knot at the end of the thread, but leave enough thread for a square knot at the end. Begin to sew at the desired knot location. Traditionally, you begin in the center sewing station so the knot is hidden on the inside. Open the book to the center spread, and follow the diagram (figure 4).

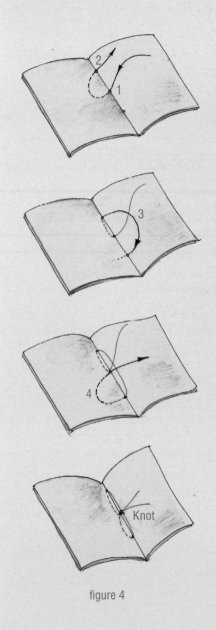

figure 4

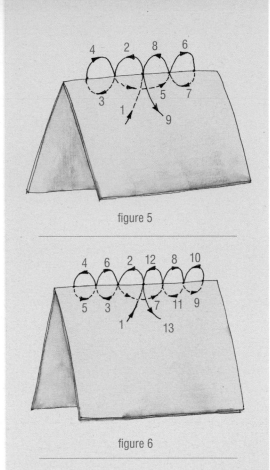

figure 5

figure 6

TIP: For a decorative touch, attach beads to the ends of the threads on the outside of the book. Begin your sewing where you want your knot to be, usually in the top station. The stitch pattern is similar to that in figure 7 except you don't skip the center hole; instead you make a figure eight in and out of the stations. Leave longer threads and attach beads to them.

Because the paper has thickness, there will be a bit of *creep* on the fore edge; the outside pages of the signature will not jut out as far as the inside ones. You can trim these pages if you want a sharp clean edge. Use a metal triangle and a cutting mat, and line the triangle up square with the top of the text block, holding the cover out of the way. If the book is thick, clamp the ruler to the table or to a board beneath the book to keep it from slipping. Use a very sharp craft knife, and hold it vertically to keep the edges of the pages aligned. Draw it along the ruler, using fairly light pressure so that the knife is cutting the paper, not shredding it. Repeat until you have cut cleanly through all the sheets.

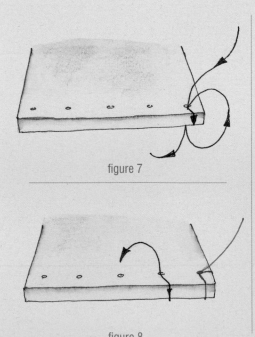

figure 7

figure 8

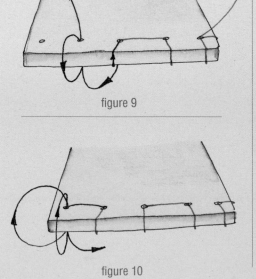

figure 9

figure 10

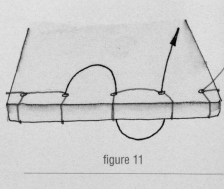

figure 11

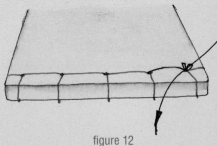

figure 12

Pamphlet Stitch, 5 or 7 hole

If the book is taller, you'll want to add more sewing stations to strengthen its structure. A basic guideline is to leave 1½ to 2 inches (3.8 to 5 cm) between the three middle holes (for a 5-hole pamphlet) and the 5 middle holes (for a 7-hole pamphlet). Note that these don't have to be evenly spaced.

For the 5-hole book, follow figure 5. For the 7-hole book (figure 6), the sewing pattern is the same, except that you add a stitch on either side as you sew. You can also begin either of these structures on the outside if you want your knot and tassel to show as part of your design.

Japanese Stab Binding

This is a good method for binding a number of single-sided sheets—collections of one-sided drawings or blank sheets for a photo album—although, as a disadvantage, it does not open flat. The stitching pattern for this book is much simpler than it looks. Using the smallest needle you can comfortably thread—it will have to go through each hole three times—and very strong thread (such as linen or strong pearl cotton), follow figures 7 through 12.

Long Stitch

This binding is fairly simple and is excellent for making a durable, multi-signature book bound to heavy paper or a piece of leather. The simple stitch pattern can be modified to make a variety of attractive designs on the spine. The following instructions are for a four-signature book, but you can use more or less depending on your needs (though three to 10 signatures is a good range).

For four signatures, you'll need a piece of thread about four times the height of the book, plus a little extra working thread. The simplest way to attach the signatures to the cover is to treat each one as a separate pamphlet, sewing it with a pamphlet stitch as shown on page 131.

Flip over and open the last signature so that its top is at the top edge of the cover, and line it up with the first set of holes (figure 13). Beginning at the foot of the book, bring the needle up through the first hole of the signature (but not the cover) leaving a tail between the cover and the text block. Then go down through the second hole of both the signature and the cover, continue up through the third hole and down through the fourth. This becomes a running stitch from bottom of the book to the top (figures 14 and 15).

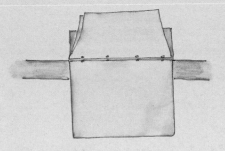

figure 13

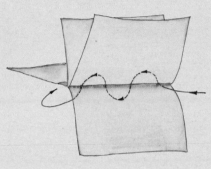

figure 14

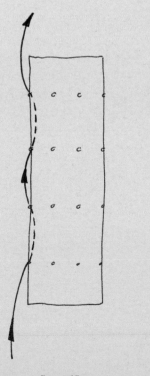

figure 15

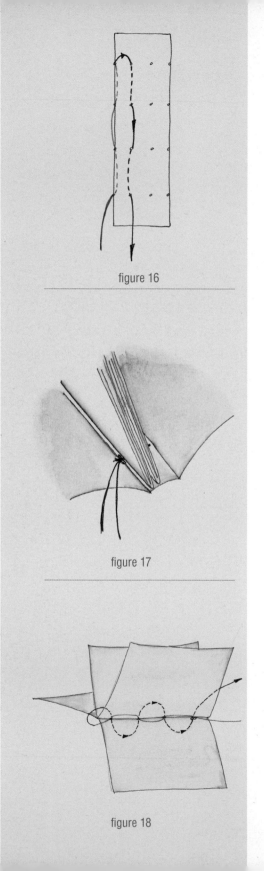

figure 16

figure 17

figure 18

Lay the next signature on top of the one you just sewed. Bring the needle up through the next hole in the top row of sewing stations in the cover, coming up through the top hole in the newly added signature. Continue down the book with a running stitch from top to bottom (figure 16). When you reach the last hole, tie the thread off with the stitch from the previous column, hiding the knot between the cover and the text block (figure 17).

Variations

For a little design interest with the long stitch, try one of these techniques, although you may need to increase the amount of thread you start with.

Try reversing the stitch pattern, filling in all the spaces between the short stitches across the top and bottom rows, with visible double threads (figures 18 and 19).

If you have fairly thin signatures, you can sew two signatures into each set of sewing stations, which will result in double stitches on the outside of the cover (figure 20).

For a more decorative finish, use a *kettle stitch* each time you come to the top and bottom signature. To do this, bring the needle under the stitch from the previous pass before going into the first hole in the next signature (figure 21). You can also do a chain stitch by going under a stitch from the previous signature, and then back into the same hole that you just came out of, making a loop that shows on the spine (figure 22).

If you want even more thread to show on the spine, continue beyond the first and last rows of holes on the spine and wrap the thread around the head and tail of the book as you stitch (figure 23).

For a book with three or more signatures, you can wrap the thread around the outside running stitches as you add the last signature, giving the spine a corded appearance. Begin by sewing the first three signatures in place. As you attach the fourth, wrap the thread around the previous two outside running stitches as you move up the book (figure 24).

If your cover material is fragile and can't withstand being punched with many sewing stations, cut slits across the rows. You will stitch through these slits in the same way that you stitch through the holes; you'll just have to adjust the placement of the stitches so that they are evenly spaced across the spine (figure 25).

Coptic Stitch

This style of binding creates a flexible book that's ideal for journals and sketchbooks since it opens flat, allowing you to easily write, draw, and paint on its pages. For a book that will travel, use strong linen thread and tough materials for the covers, or reinforce the sewing stations on the cover with small metal eyelets.

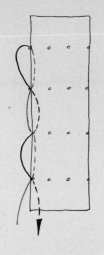

figure 19

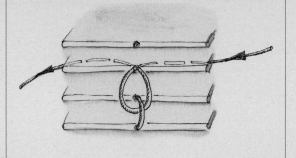

figure 22

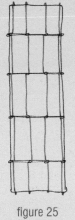

figure 25

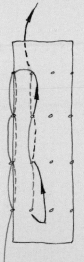

figure 20

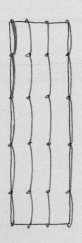

figure 23

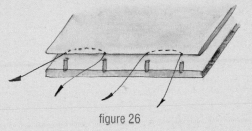

figure 26

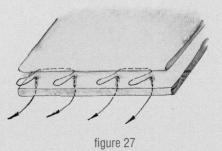

figure 27

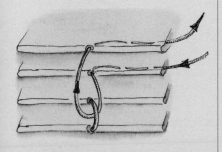

figure 21

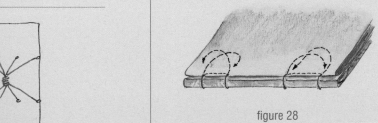

figure 24

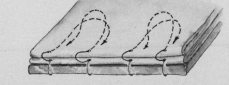

figure 28

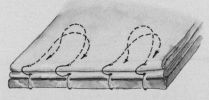

figure 29

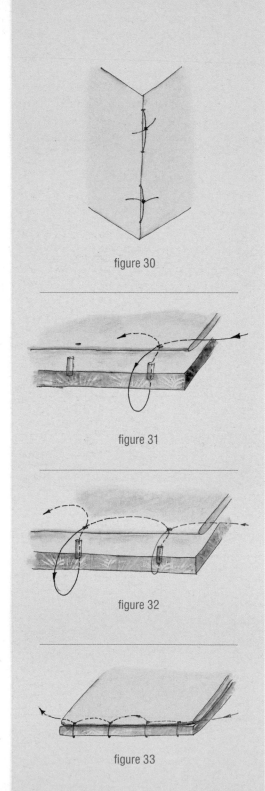

figure 30

figure 31

figure 32

figure 33

To have the most design options for the spine, use six to 10 signatures, keeping in mind that the sewing stations do not need to be evenly spaced.

Multi-Needle Coptic Stitch

This structure is the simplest, although you'll have to keep track of a number of needles. Depending on the height of the book, you can work with two, four, or six sets of holes. These directions are for four holes; modify them for either two or six holes.

Thread a needle on each end of a long thread, about 30 inches (76.2 cm) or so. Lock the thread in place and complete the following steps. Place the last signature of the book on the cover, with the spine facing you. Open the signature and bring each of the needles out through a hole, evening up the tails so that you have equal lengths of thread hanging from each hole (figure 26).

Attach the cover by going through the hole nearest to each dangling thread; then come back up and go back through the same hole in the signature that you just exited (figure 27). The needles will now change positions, so the needle that just came out of station number one will go back down through station number two and vice versa. Repeat for stations three and four (figure 28).

Take the needle at the first station back towards the cover and make a kettle stitch (page 134) by inserting it under the stitch between the signature and the cover, bringing it back to the outside; repeat this step at each station. Add the next signature to the book, and bring the needle towards the same station in that signature, pulling the thread snugly. Repeat this for each station (figure 29). Switch places with the needles as you did above, coming out of alternate stations.

Add the cover to the book by bringing each needle through the station on the cover. Then bring the needles back to make a kettle stitch beneath the last signature and into its inside. Tie the threads in square knots in the spaces between station numbers one and two, and again between three and four (figure 30).

Single-Needle Coptic Stitch

This technique is a bit different in that you'll use a single thread, moving up and down the spine and in and out of each set of stations.

With the spine facing you, place the last signature of the book on the back cover, again with the spine facing you. Beginning at station one inside the signature, bring the needle to the outside and then up through the first hole in the cover (figure 31). Leave a tail of about three inches (7.6 cm) inside the signature. Go back into the first signature—pulling the threads snug but being careful not to tear the paper—move to the second station, and repeat the step (figure 32). Continue to work your way across the spine, going down through each station and then back up again (figure 33).

When you have come out of station four, add another signature and come up inside the fourth station on that signature (figure 34). Work your way back to the opposite end of the book, attaching this second signature. As you come down out of the end stations at the head and tail of the book, make a kettle stitch (page 134) by slipping the needle under the connecting stitch between the first signature and the cover, bringing it again to the outside, and then going back into the station in the next signature. For the second and third stations, make a chain stitch (page 134) by making a loop under the stitch from the previous row, and then going back into the hole you just exited (figure 35).

When you get back to the first station, secure the tail you left at the beginning by going up through the first hole of the first signature and tie a square knot. Then come back out of this signature. Make a kettle stitch. Add the third signature to the book; bring the needle up into the first station in this signature (figure 36). Repeat this stitch pattern, working up and down the spine of the book and adding signatures as you get to each end.

Attach the cover and the last signature at the same time by repeating the process you used at the beginning: come out of each station, make a kettle stitch with the signature below, and then attach the cover by going through the holes in the cover. When you have sewn through all the stations, bring the thread back to the inside of the last signature, and tie a pair of slip knots under the last running stitch in the center of this signature. Trim the threads to about a ½ inch (1.3 cm) (figure 37).

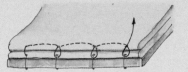

figure 34

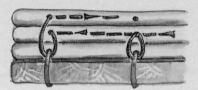

figure 35

figure 36

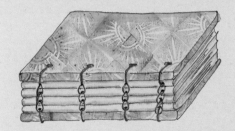

figure 37

templates

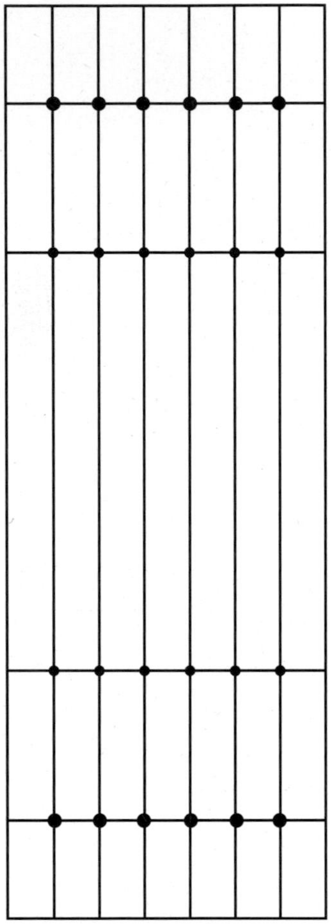

Cereal Box Books Spine

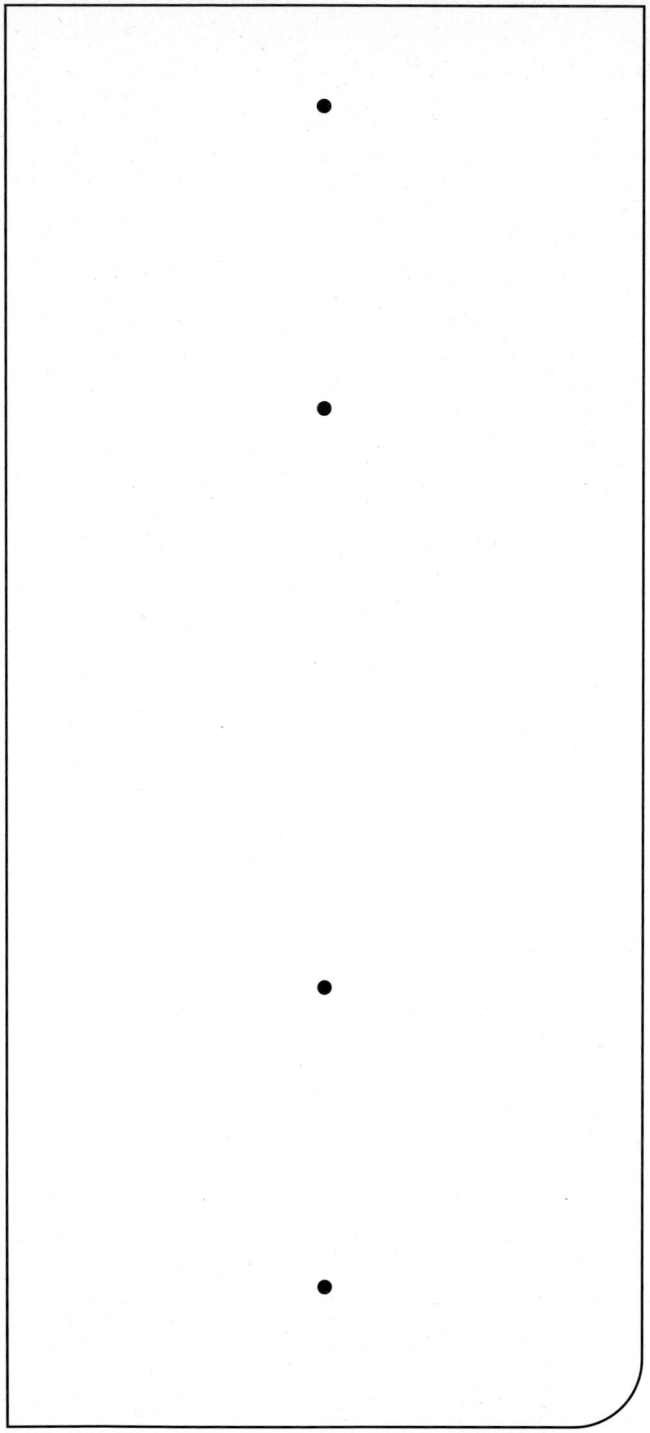

Mousepad Journal

Shopper's Joy Book Spine

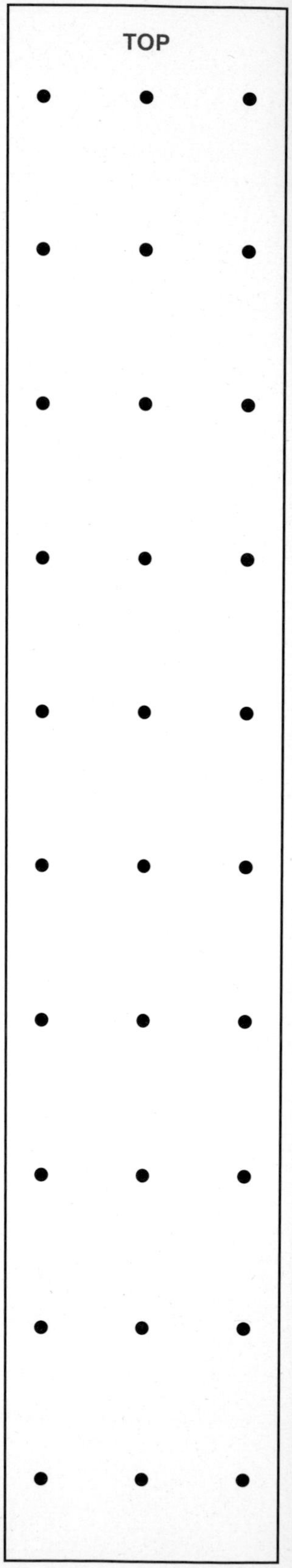

TOP

Journey Journal

Slinky Map Book

Shopper's Joy Book Signature

Cereal Box Books Signature

6"/15.2 cm

6"/15.2 cm

5¹/₂"/14 cm

Spine

3¹/₂"/8.9 cm

4¹/₂"/11.4 cm

4"/10.2 cm

Weatherproof Journal foldout page (shown at 35%)

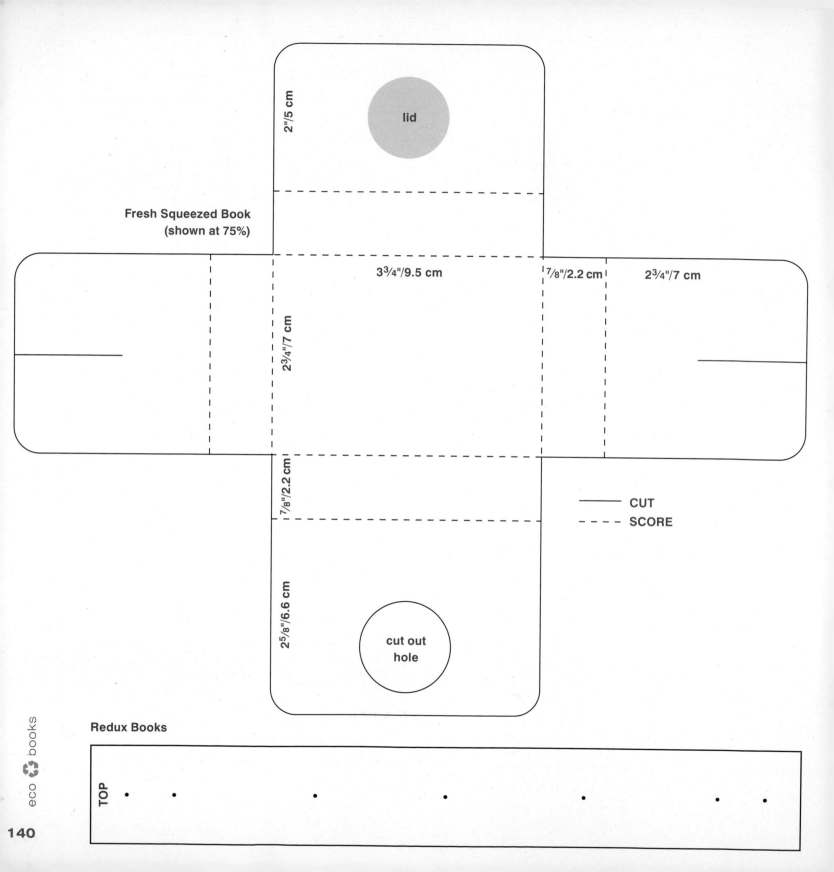

Fresh Squeezed Book
(shown at 75%)

lid

2"/5 cm

3¾"/9.5 cm

⁷⁄₈"/2.2 cm

2¾"/7 cm

2¾"/7 cm

⁷⁄₈"/2.2 cm

2⁵⁄₈"/6.6 cm

cut out
hole

——— CUT

- - - SCORE

Redux Books

TOP

about the designers

Margaret Couch Cogswell
Margaret has been making books for over 12 years. Although she has worked with a variety of mediums over time, her conviction that our greatest rewards often come from simple, everyday objects has been a constant. Margaret has a B.A. from Rhodes College and has also attended Rhode Island School of Design, Arrowmont School of Arts and Crafts, and Penland School of Crafts, where she is currently a resident artist.

Heather Crossley
Heather is a self-experimental mixed-media artist. Her work has appeared in numerous United States and Australian magazines and books, such as *500 Handmade Books*, *Artful Paper Dolls*, and *Rubber Stamped Jewelry*. Heather has also been featured on the covers of *Somerset Studio*, *Stamper's Sampler*, *Stamping and Papercraft*, *Australian Paper Arts*, and the *Rubber Gazette*. Originally from Singapore, Heather now lives, works, and plays in Brisbane, Australia. (http://homepage.powerup.com.au/~mkhc).

Donna J. Engstrom
Donna is a mixed-media artist who loves to combine paint, collage, and found objects. Donna has a sinfully large collection of found object treasures. Her goal is to elevate appreciation for these ordinary objects by highlighting them in her work. Donna has been featured in several Somerset Studio publications and teaches classes and workshops on collage and assemblage. (www.donna-engstrom-abstract-art.com).

Michelle Francis
By day, Michelle works as a mild-mannered archivist, but at night she transforms into a crazed book artist. Michelle enjoys the challenge of melding an idea into a book form that both invites and informs the beholder. She lives in Asheville, North Carolina, with her husband, Hal Keiner, a letterpress printer. They recently became proud new parents to Van der Cook, IV. Life won't ever be the same again.

Reiko Fujii
As a mixed-media artist, Reiko inherited her grandmother's tendency to reuse newspaper, cardboard, and oddly shaped containers. Reiko earned a B.A. in psychology from the University of California, Berkeley. Later, at the age of 54, she received her M.F.A. from John F. Kennedy University. Her handmade books can be found in private collections and in the Mills College Library Special Collection.

Leslie Hart
Leslie is a secretary by day and re-creator by night. She lives by a small lake with her husband, two dogs, and a cat. Give her a piece of trash and she might be wearing it the next day. Leslie's favorite cake is carrot cake, she doesn't have a lucky number, and she hopes to win the lottery some day. Leslie's other passion is mail art. (www.snailmailart.blogspot.com; www.thegreenwardrobe.etsy.com)

Michael A. Henninger
Michael A. Henninger has made book art since 1988 under the Rat Art Press imprint. He also teaches bookmaking, printmaking, and digital art at California State University, East Bay. He is often able to re-use materials from his other pursuits (like enjoying a good beer) in his books. Among other things, he has an interest in advertising graphics, package art, and product design. (www.ratartpress.com).

Sara Hindmarch
Sara Hindmarch works full time in the museum business. Whatever time she has left over goes to hackbooking and photography, or to playing with her Corgi-Chihuahua mix, Clementine. Hackbooking is her bit of jargon for the craft of guerilla bookbinding using found objects and fine papers in combination with traditional bookbinding and scrapbooking tools. Sara lives with her husband in Atlanta, Georgia. (http://www.re-paper.net)

Julie Gray
After a career in commercial art, business, and publishing, Julie Gray spends time now as a calligrapher and bookmaker. Julie has a B.A. from the Columbus College of Art & Design in Ohio. Her work can be found in handmade book, greeting card, envelope, and Artist Trading Card exchanges, as well as *Bound & Lettered*, the *2004 Calligraphers Engagement Calendar*, *Somerset Studio*, and various exhibits. Julie lives, loves, and letters in Albuquerque, New Mexico.

Karen J. Lauseng
Karen is a studio artist working in Silver City, New Mexico. She has a B.S. in Economics and B.F.A. and M.F.A. degrees in metalsmithing from Kansas State University. Karen's artwork has been exhibited widely and showcased in various national and international magazines including *Art Jewelry*, *Lapidary Journal/Jewelry Artist*, *The Crafts Report*, and *Creative Home Arts*. Her creative designs have been presented in numerous Lark Book publications. (www.kjartworks.com).

Annie Fain Liden
Annie Fain grew up in a family of craftspeople, sheep farmers, and musicians. Five years ago she established A. Fain Books in Asheville, North Carolina, where she makes custom journals, sketchbooks, and wedding books. Annie Fain is known to sneak fiber arts techniques, particularly hand-embroidery, into her book designs and is a great believer in the blank book as a place to explore personal creativity. (www.afainbooks.com).

Bob Meadows
Now retired from more than 40 years as a graphic designer, Bob devotes most of his time to creating artists' books. Bob teaches bookmaking and paper transformation in Knoxville, Tennessee, and at the John C. Campbell Folk School. Bob is a member of the Foothills Craft Guild, Tennessee Book Arts Guild, and Knoxville Book Arts Guild.

Geri Michelli
Geri is a member of LIBROS: New Mexico Book Arts Guild, as well as the Book Arts Group of Santa Fe, and has participated in annual collaborative books as well as group exhibitions. Geri is a substitute teacher in the Rio Rancho Public Schools and has conducted many bookmaking workshops for students of all ages. She currently lives in the high desert of Rio Rancho, New Mexico, with her husband and two sons.

Rhonda Miller
Rhonda is a bookbinder and book artist in Nova Scotia, Canada. She was sidetracked from librarianship when she started taking bookbinding classes about six years ago. Rhonda does a lot of work with leather and traditional hardcover bindings. She then uses the scrap materials to make green books as often as possible. Rhonda also does papermaking, paper marbling, paste papers, printmaking, and box making. (www.MyHandboundBooks.com).

Cassie Ogle
In 2006, Cassie received a Handmade in America grant to participate in a hand-bound book apprenticeship at Southwest Virginia Community College. Cassie uses traditional crafting skills to create out-of-the-ordinary, yet practical things. Part of her creative process is coming up with ways to use materials that are not typically used in bookmaking. When she is not making books, Cassie knits, crochets, and spins wool. She lives in Richlands, Virginia. (http://www.thecraftykitten.com; http://paperkitty.wordpress.com).

Alexia Petrakos
Alexia Petrakos has been a paper geek ever since she was a little girl. Alexia is mostly self-taught and has been binding books for six years. In addition to bookbinding, Alexia makes websites, sews, sculpts, creates mixed-media art in her art journals and on canvas, and tries just about anything else she finds interesting. Alexia lives with her husband in Atlanta, Georgia. (http://www.imakearrrt.com; http://www.thealternatingcurent.com; http://www.waitcomeback.com)

Nancy Pobanz
Nancy was raised in Oregon by a mom who taught her children to reduce, re-use, and recycle before the phrase was invented. In the 1980s, Nancy lived in the Philippines where she learned to improvise with scarce art supplies. She continued making many of her supplies in graduate school. Now she regularly returns to Oregon's high desert, where she gathers rock to grind into pigment and plants for cordage or papermaking. (www.nancypobanz.com)

Geraldine Pomeroy
Geraldine has explored and created in several mediums for over 22 years. She has taught many workshops at art centers, art festivals, and universities. Her works are an homage to nature—not as something separate from us, but as something intrinsically entwined with us. Geraldine creates her work in a studio in a lush green valley of the Strzelecki Ranges in Victoria, Australia. (www.geocities.com/wildfibres)

Cheryl Prose
Cheryl is cofounder of the Knoxville Book Arts Guild. She is fortunate to have taken classes taught by outstanding teachers such as Dan Essig, Shanna Leino, Laurie Corral, Bob Meadows, and Bob Roberts.

Mary Ann Sampson
Mary Ann lives in rural Alabama and has a studio, The One-Eye Opera Co., in an old renovated bank. She began making unique books during the mid-80s. Mary Ann has taught the palm-leaf prayer book structure in workshops at the University of Alabama, Penland School of Crafts, and Paper and Book Intensive. Her work has appeared in *Making Memory Books by Hand* and *500 Handmade Books* (2008, Lark). (www.vampandtramp.com)

Gail Stiffe
Gail discovered hand papermaking in the early 1980s and then began bookbinding as a way to present her work. Gail uses materials from a local organization that sells industrial waste that would otherwise go to the landfill. She has held several solo exhibitions and has participated in group shows in Australia and overseas. Gail is the current editor of the International Paper Association and convenes the Australian Women's Art Register. (www.gailstiffe.info; www.papergail.blogspot.com)

Maura Toledo
By day, Mauro is a mild-mannered advertising art director. By night, he is a passionate bookbinder, spending most of his time cutting paper and gluing items together for his books. He graduated from Art Center College of Design in 1999. Mauro has a unique desire for repurposing beautiful things that other people would throw out. He lives in Long Beach, California, with his wife and two small dogs.

Erin Zamrzla
Erin Zamrzla was born in Kansas and has spent most of her life there, earning B.F.A. and M.F.A. degrees in graphic design from Fort Hays State University. Erin's favorite part of bookmaking is the combination of working with paper and found objects. She especially enjoys transforming old used objects into something new and wonderful. She currently designs, paints, and binds books from her home in Santa Monica, California. (www.erinzam.com)

about the author

Terry Taylor is a senior editor at Lark Books. He's the author of several books including *The Artful Storybook* (Lark Books, 2008), *Altered Art* (Lark Books, 2004), *Artful Paper Dolls* (Lark Books, 2006), and *The Artful Object* (Lark Books, 2006). He's a jeweler in his spare time and prefers to spend his vacation time taking metalworking classes. His other passion requires him to fly around the country to see well-known opera companies perform.

acknowledgments

Thanks to Deborah Morgenthal, whose off-the-top-of-her-head idea was the seed for this book. And, even more importantly, many thanks to Amanda Carestio and Beth Sweet whose enthusiasm and energy for the book made it a reality.

index of gallery artists

index